北京大学中国语言学研究中心

早期北京话珍稀文献集成

主编 刘云

西人北京话教科书汇编

分卷主编 翟赟 郭利霞 陈颖

汉语口语初级读本
北京儿歌

[意] 威达雷 编著

图书在版编目(CIP)数据

汉语口语初级读本. 北京儿歌 /(意) 威达雷编著. —影印本. —北京：北京大学出版社，2017.8
（早期北京话珍本典籍校释与研究）
ISBN 978-7-301-28587-9

Ⅰ.①汉… Ⅱ.①威… Ⅲ.①汉语—口语—对外汉语教学—教材 Ⅳ.①H195.4

中国版本图书馆CIP数据核字(2017)第195701号

书　　名	汉语口语初级读本·北京儿歌（影印本） HANYU KOUYU CHUJI DUBEN·BEIJING ERGE（YINGYINBEN）
著作责任者	［意］威达雷　编著
责任编辑	王禾雨　宋立文
标准书号	ISBN 978-7-301-28587-9
出版发行	北京大学出版社
地　　址	北京市海淀区成府路205号　100871
网　　址	http://www.pup.cn　　新浪微博：@北京大学出版社
电子信箱	zpup@pup.cn
电　　话	邮购部 62752015　发行部 62750672　编辑部 62753374
印 刷 者	北京京华虎彩印刷有限公司
经 销 者	新华书店
	720毫米×1020毫米　16开本　24.25印张　177千字 2017年8月第1版　2018年3月第2次印刷
定　　价	93.00元

未经许可，不得以任何方式复制或抄袭本书之部分或全部内容。
版权所有，侵权必究
举报电话: 010-62752024　电子信箱: fd@pup.pku.edu.cn
图书如有印装质量问题，请与出版部联系，电话: 010-62756370

基督新教来华传教士汉语研究著述考
（14BZJ022，2014年国家社会科学基金项目）

总　序

　　语言是文化的重要组成部分，也是文化的载体。语言中有历史。

　　多元一体的中华文化，体现在我国丰富的民族文化和地域文化及其语言和方言之中。

　　北京是辽金元明清五代国都（辽时为陪都），千余年来，逐渐成为中华民族所公认的政治中心。北方多个少数民族文化与汉文化在这里碰撞、融合，产生出以汉文化为主体的、带有民族文化风味的特色文化。

　　现今的北京话是我国汉语方言和地域文化中极具特色的一支，它与辽金元明四代的北京话是否有直接继承关系还不是十分清楚。但可以肯定的是，它与清代以来旗人语言文化与汉人语言文化的彼此交融有直接关系。再往前追溯，旗人与汉人语言文化的接触与交融在入关前已经十分深刻。本丛书收集整理的这些语料直接反映了清代以来北京话、京味儿文化的发展变化。

　　早期北京话有独特的历史传承和文化底蕴，于中华文化、历史有特别的意义。

　　一者，这一时期的北京历经满汉双语共存、双语互协而新生出的汉语方言——北京话，它最终成为我国民族共同语（普通话）的基础方言。这一过程是中华多元一体文化自然形成的诸过程之一，对于了解形成中华文化多元一体关系的具体进程有重要的价值。

　　二者，清代以来，北京曾历经数次重要的社会变动：清王朝的逐渐孱弱、八国联军的入侵、帝制覆灭和民国建立及其伴随的满汉关系变化、各路军阀的来来往往、日本侵略者的占领等等。在这些不同的社会环境下，北京人的构成有无重要变化？北京话和京味儿文化是否有变化？进一步地，地域方言和文化与自身的传承性或发展性有着什么样的关系？与社会变迁有着什么样的关系？清代以至民国时期早期北京话的语料为研究语言文化自身传承性与社会的关系提供了很好的素材。

　　了解历史才能更好地把握未来。中华人民共和国成立后,北京不仅是全国的政治中心,而且是全国的文化和科研中心,新的北京话和京味儿文化或正在形成。什么是老北京京味儿文化的精华?如何传承这些精华?为把握新的地域文化形成的规律,为传承地域文化的精华,必须对过去的地域文化的特色及其形成过程进行细致的研究和理性的分析。而近几十年来,各种新的传媒形式不断涌现,外来西方文化和国内其他地域文化的冲击越来越强烈,北京地区人口流动日趋频繁,老北京人逐渐分散,老北京话已几近消失。清代以来各个重要历史时期早期北京话语料的保护整理和研究迫在眉睫。

　　"早期北京话珍本典籍校释与研究(暨早期北京话文献数字化工程)"是北京大学中国语言学研究中心研究成果,由"早期北京话珍稀文献集成""早期北京话数据库"和"早期北京话研究书系"三部分组成。"集成"收录从清中叶到民国末年反映早期北京话面貌的珍稀文献并对内容加以整理,"数据库"为研究者分析语料提供便利,"研究书系"是在上述文献和数据库基础上对早期北京话的集中研究,反映了当前相关研究的最新进展。

　　本丛书可以为语言学、历史学、社会学、民俗学、文化学等多方面的研究提供素材。

　　愿本丛书的出版为中华优秀文化的传承做出贡献!

王洪君、郭锐、刘云
2016年10月

"早期北京话珍稀文献集成"序

　　清民两代是北京话走向成熟的关键阶段。从汉语史的角度看，这是一个承前启后的重要时期，而成熟后的北京话又开始为当代汉民族共同语——普通话源源不断地提供着养分。蒋绍愚先生对此有着深刻的认识："特别是清初到19世纪末这一段的汉语，虽然按分期来说是属于现代汉语而不属于近代汉语，但这一段的语言（语法，尤其是词汇）和'五四'以后的语言（通常所说的'现代汉语'就是指'五四'以后的语言）还有若干不同，研究这一段语言对于研究近代汉语是如何发展到'五四'以后的语言是很有价值的。"（《近代汉语研究概要》，北京大学出版社，2005年）然而国内的早期北京话研究并不尽如人意，在重视程度和材料发掘力度上都要落后于日本同行。自1876年至1945年间，日本汉语教学的目的语转向当时的北京话，因此留下了大批的北京话教材，这为其早期北京话研究提供了材料支撑。作为日本北京话研究的奠基者，太田辰夫先生非常重视新语料的发掘，很早就利用了《小额》《北京》等京味儿小说材料。这种治学理念得到了很好的传承，之后，日本陆续影印出版了《中国语学资料丛刊》《中国语教本类集成》《清民语料》等资料汇编，给研究带来了便利。

　　新材料的发掘是学术研究的源头活水。陈寅恪《〈敦煌劫余录〉序》有云："一时代之学术，必有其新材料与新问题。取用此材料，以研求问题，则为此时代学术之新潮流。"我们的研究要想取得突破，必须打破材料桎梏。在具体思路上，一方面要拓展视野，关注"异族之故书"，深度利用好朝鲜、日本、泰西诸国作者所主导编纂的早期北京话教本；另一方面，更要利用本土优势，在"吾国之旧籍"中深入挖掘，官话正音教本、满汉合璧教本、京味儿小说、曲艺剧本等新类型语料大有文章可做。在明确了思路之后，我们从2004年开始了前期的准备工作，在北京大学中国语言学研究中心的大力支持下，早期北京话的挖掘整理工作于2007年正式启动。本次推出的"早期北京话珍稀文献集成"是阶段性成果之一，总体设计上"取异族之故书与吾国之旧籍互相补正"，共分"日本北京话教科书汇编""朝鲜日据时期汉语会话书汇编""西人北京话教科书汇编""清代满汉合璧文献萃编""清代官话正音文献""十全福""清末民初京味儿小说书系""清末民初京味儿时评书系"八个系列，胪列如下：

"日本北京话教科书汇编"于日本早期北京话会话书、综合教科书、改编读物和风俗纪闻读物中精选出《燕京妇语》《四声联珠》《华语跬步》《官话指南》《改订官话指南》《亚细亚言语集》《京华事略》《北京纪闻》《北京风土编》《北京风俗问答》《北京事情》《伊苏普喻言》《搜奇新编》《今古奇观》等二十余部作品。这些教材是日本早期北京话教学活动的缩影，也是研究早期北京方言、民俗、史地问题的宝贵资料。本系列的编纂得到了日本学界的大力帮助。冰野善宽、内田庆市、太田斋、鳟泽彰夫诸先生在书影拍摄方面给予了诸多帮助。书中日语例言、日语小引的翻译得到了竹越孝先生的悉心指导，在此深表谢忱。

"朝鲜日据时期汉语会话书汇编"由韩国著名汉学家朴在渊教授和金雅瑛博士校注，收入《改正增补汉语独学》《修正独习汉语指南》《高等官话华语精选》《官话华语教范》《速修汉语自通》《速修汉语大成》《无先生速修中国语自通》《官话标准：短期速修中国语自通》《中语大全》《"内鲜满"最速成中国语自通》等十余部日据时期（1910年至1945年）朝鲜教材。这批教材既是对《老乞大》《朴通事》的传承，又深受日本早期北京话教学活动的影响。在中韩语言史、文化史研究中，日据时期是近现代过渡的重要时期，这些资料具有多方面的研究价值。

"西人北京话教科书汇编"收录了《语言自迩集》《官话类编》等十余部西人编纂教材。这些西方作者多受过语言学训练，他们用印欧语的眼光考量汉语，解释汉语语法现象，设计记音符号系统，对早期北京话语音、词汇、语法面貌的描写要比本土文献更为精准。感谢郭锐老师提供了《官话类编》《北京话语音读本》和《汉语口语初级读本》的底本，《寻津录》、《语言自迩集》（第一版、第二版）、《汉英北京官话词汇》、《华语入门》等底本由北京大学图书馆特藏部提供,谨致谢忱。《华英文义津逮》《言语声片》为笔者从海外购回,其中最为珍贵的是老舍先生在伦敦东方学院执教期间,与英国学者共同编写的教材——《言语声片》。教材共分两卷:第一卷为英文卷,用英语讲授汉语,用音标标注课文的读音;第二卷为汉字卷。《言语声片》采用先用英语导入,再学习汉字的教学方法讲授汉语口语,是世界上第一部有声汉语教材。书中汉字均由老舍先生亲笔书写,全书由老舍先生录音,共十六张唱片,京韵十足,殊为珍贵。

上述三类"异族之故书"经江蓝生、张卫东、汪维辉、张美兰、李无未、王顺洪、张西平、鲁健骥、王澧华诸先生介绍,已经进入学界视野,对北京话研究和对外汉语教学史研究产生了很大的推动作用。我们希望将更多的域外经典北京话教本引入进来,考虑到日本卷和朝鲜卷中很多抄本字迹潦草,难以辨认,而刻本、印本中也存在着大量的异体字和俗字,重排点校注释的出版形式更利于研究者利用,这也是前文"深度利用"的含义所在。

对"吾国之旧籍"挖掘整理的成果,则体现在下面五个系列中:

"清代满汉合璧文献萃编"收入《清文启蒙》《清话问答四十条》《清文指要》《续编兼汉清文指要》《庸言知旨》《满汉成语对待》《清文接字》《重刻清文虚字指南编》等十余部经典满汉合璧文献。入关以后,在汉语这一强势语言的影响下,熟习满语的满人越来越少,故雍正以降,出现了一批用当时的北京话注释翻译的满语会话书和语法书。这批教科书的目的本是教授旗人学习满语,却无意中成为了早期北京话的珍贵记录。"清代满汉合璧文献萃编"首次对这批文献进行了大规模整理,不仅对北京话溯源和满汉语言接触研究具有重要意义,也将为满语研究和满语教学创造极大便利。由于底本多为善本古籍,研究者不易见到,在北京大学图书馆古籍部和日本神户市外国语大学竹越孝教授的大力协助下,"萃编"将以重排点校加影印的形式出版。

"清代官话正音文献"收入《正音撮要》(高静亭著)和《正音咀华》(莎彝尊著)两种代表著作。雍正六年(1728),雍正谕令福建、广东两省推行官话,福建为此还专门设立了正音书馆。这一"正音"运动的直接影响就是以《正音撮要》和《正音咀华》为代表的一批官话正音教材的问世。这些书的作者或为旗人,或寓居京城多年,书中保留着大量北京话词汇和口语材料,具有极高的研究价值。沈国威先生和侯兴泉先生对底本搜集助力良多,特此致谢。

《十全福》是北京大学图书馆藏《程砚秋玉霜簃戏曲珍本》之一种,为同治元年陈金雀抄本。陈晓博士发现该传奇虽为昆腔戏,念白却多为京话,较为罕见。

以上三个系列均为古籍,且不乏善本,研究者不容易接触到,因此我们提供了影印全文。

总体来说,由于言文不一,清代的本土北京话语料数量较少。而到了清末民初,风气渐开,情况有了很大变化。彭翼仲、文实权、蔡友梅等一批北京爱国知识分子通过开办白话报来"开启民智""改良社会"。著名爱国报人彭翼仲在《京话日报》的发刊词中这样写道:"本报为输进文明、改良风俗,以开通社会多数人之智识为宗旨。故通幅概用京话,以浅显之笔,达朴实之理,纪紧要之事,务令雅俗共赏,妇稚咸宜。"在当时北京白话报刊的诸多栏目中,最受市民欢迎的当属京味儿小说连载和《益世余谭》之类的评论栏目,语言极为地道。

"清末民初京味儿小说书系"首次对以蔡友梅、冷佛、徐剑胆、儒丐、勋锐为代表的晚清民国京味儿作家群及作品进行系统挖掘和整理,从千余部京味儿小说中萃取代表作家的代表作品,并加以点校注释。该作家群活跃于清末民初,以报纸为阵地,以小说为工具,开展了一场轰轰烈烈的底层启蒙运动,为新文化运动的兴起打下了一定的群众基础,他们的作品对老舍等京味儿小说大家的创作产生了积极影响。本系列的问世亦将为文学史和思想史研究提供议题。于润琦、方梅、陈清茹、雷晓彤诸先生为本系列提供了部分底本或馆藏线索,首都图书馆历史文献阅览室、天津图书馆、国家图书馆提供了极大便利,谨致谢意!

"清末民初京味儿时评书系"则收入《益世余谭》和《益世余墨》,均系著名京味儿小说家蔡友梅在民初报章上发表的专栏时评,由日本岐阜圣德学园大学刘一之教授、矢野贺子教授校注。

这一时期存世的报载北京话语料口语化程度高,且总量庞大,但发掘和整理却殊为不易,称得上"珍稀"二字。一方面,由于报载小说等栏目的流行,外地作者也加入了京味儿小说创作行列,五花八门的笔名背后还需考证作者是否为京籍，以蔡友梅为例，其真名为蔡松龄，查明的笔名还有损、损公、退化、亦我、梅蒐、老梅、今睿等。另一方面，这些作者的作品多为急就章，文字错讹很多，并且鲜有单行本存世，老报纸残损老化的情况日益严重，整理的难度可想而知。

上述八个系列在某种程度上填补了相关领域的空白。由于各个系列在内容、体例、出版年代和出版形式上都存在较大的差异，我们在整理时借鉴《朝鲜时代汉语教科书丛刊续编》《〈清文指要〉汇校与语言研究》等语言类古籍的整理体例，结合各个系列自身特点和读者需求，灵活制定体例。"清末民初京味儿小说书系"和"清末民初京味儿时评书系"年代较近，读者群体更为广泛，经过多方调研和反复讨论，我们决定在整理时使用简体横排的形式，尽可能同时满足专业研究者和普通读者的需求。"清代满汉合璧文献萃编""清代官话正音文献"等系列整理时则采用繁体。"早期北京话珍稀文献集成"总计六十余册，总字数近千万字，称得上是工程浩大，由于我们能力有限，体例和校注中难免会有疏漏，加之受客观条件所限，一些拟定的重要书目本次无法收入，还望读者多多谅解。

"早期北京话珍稀文献集成"可以说是中日韩三国学者通力合作的结晶，得到了方方面面的帮助，我们还要感谢陆俭明、马真、蒋绍愚、江蓝生、崔希亮、方梅、张美兰、陈前瑞、赵日新、陈跃红、徐大军、张世方、李明、邓如冰、王强、陈保新诸先生的大力支持，感谢北京大学图书馆的协助以及萧群书记的热心协调。"集成"的编纂队伍以青年学者为主，经验不足，两位丛书总主编倾注了大量心血。王洪君老师不仅在经费和资料上提供保障，还积极扶掖新进，"我们搭台，你们年轻人唱戏"的话语令人倍感温暖和鼓舞。郭锐老师在经费和人员上也予以了大力支持，不仅对体例制定、底本选定等具体工作进行了细致指导，还无私地将自己发现的新材料和新课题与大家分享，令人钦佩。"集成"能够顺利出版还要特别感谢国家出版基金规划管理办公室的支持以及北京大学出版社王明舟社长、张凤珠副总编的精心策划，感谢汉语编辑室杜若明、邓晓霞、张弘泓、宋立文等老师所付出的辛劳。需要感谢的师友还有很多，在此一并致以诚挚的谢意。

"上穷碧落下黄泉，动手动脚找东西"，我们不奢望引领"时代学术之新潮流",惟愿能给研究者带来一些便利,免去一些奔波之苦,这也是我们向所有关心帮助过"早期北京话珍稀文献集成"的人士致以的最诚挚的谢意。

刘 云

2015年6月23日

于对外经贸大学求索楼

2016年4月19日

改定于润泽公馆

《汉语口语初级读本》导读

李海英

近30年来,随着中外文化交流的日益加强,海外的汉语教学研究持续升温,已经成为一门重要的学科。在国内,晚清以来西方外交官所编写的汉语读本,连同来华传教士所编写的汉语教材,已成为汉语学界和文化研究领域关注的热点。在中西文化交流史上,民国以前的西方汉语教学大致由传教士、外交官、来华商人等几类人主导。不容否认,西方来华外交官代表西方国家的强权利益,但在文化交流方面他们也并非全无是处。比如,意大利外交官威达雷曾就1896年之前流行于中国北方的官话童谣进行过认真的整理,编译而成汉语读本《北京儿歌》(*Pekinese Rhymes*,1896);1901年出版了由99篇中国传统寓言笑话改编而成的《汉语口语初级读本》(*A First Reading Book for Students of Colloquial Chinese*,1901),两本书都保留了北京方言的诸多特点。作为中西文化交流的产物,这两本书不仅对二十世纪二三十年代以后的中国民俗研究产生过相当大的影响,也是国内外学术界研究晚清北京语言和社会风貌的珍贵文献资料。

一、关于作者威达雷

意大利外交官威达雷(Guido Amedeo Vitale,1872—1918,亦译卫太尔、韦大列),曾于1893—1899年(清光绪年间)任意大利驻华使馆翻译(1896—1897年间兼代办),1899—1915任汉文正使。威达雷的老师是意大利教授诺全提尼(Lodovico Nocentini,1849—1910),诺全提尼曾于1883年被派驻上海领事馆，是第一位以"实习口译员"身份在中国生活过的意大利教授，五年后回国继续担任罗马大学中文教授。《北京儿歌》第一版的扉页上，威达雷就表达了对老师诺全提尼的敬重和友情。威达雷语言才能卓越，中文发音几近完美，深受当时意大利驻华大使的赏识，据说连慈禧太后也非常欣赏他（图莉安 2007）。威达雷的学术成就主要表现在汉语读本的研究和整理上，其作品包括上面提到的《北京儿歌》和《汉语口语初级读本》等。中国人对这两部作品赞誉有加，比如胡适等人发起的文学改革运动，就从中汲取了灵感。另外，威达雷与人合写的《蒙古语文法及字典》（*Grammaire et vocabulaire de la langue mongole, dialecte des Khalkhas*）也是其学术水准的极好证明，该书于1897年在北京出版。1899年3月，威达雷获法国政府授勋"银棕榈"，并被命为"学院骑士"（图莉安 2007）。

本书所选的威达雷的两部汉语著作，各有其特点。如果说童谣集《北京儿歌》是威达雷所收集的中国民间故事的零散碎片，是其为了帮助外国人了解中国的采风之作的话，《汉语口语初级读本》则是他精心甄选编译，为来华西方人学习汉语官话服务的真正意义上的口语读本。因本丛书重点是汉语教材，故将早出版的《北京儿歌》排在《汉语口语初级读本》之后。

二、《汉语口语初级读本》的成书背景及体例

《汉语口语初级读本》，又译为《北京笑话》，1901年由北堂印书社出版。作者在初版序中提到，该书的99篇笑话毫无疑问属于民间故事，但是在中国，每一位读书人对于汉语口语有一种天然的厌恶，以致他选编的那些广为人知且被广泛引用的篇目只是以书面语的方式存在。因此，威达雷从几千篇作品中挑选出这些笑话来并将其译成官话，他希望那些学习汉语口语的人能够从这些日常课文阅读中受益，能从中感受到欢乐，从而减轻他们学习汉

语时的痛苦和沉闷。

《汉语口语初级读本》由索引和正文两个部分构成。索引包括99篇中国传统笑话的英文译名和各篇目的页码，按先后顺序横排印刷，借鉴了当时教会编写汉语教材的编排方式。正文则完全为用官话写成的99个笑话。每一篇笑话标题前有序号，另行接下来是笑话全文。正文自右向左竖行编排，采用了中国传统的编排方式，文中只有句读，没有采用新式的标点符号。

三、《汉语口语初级读本》的特色与价值

（一）用浅近的北京话向西方介绍了中国的寓言笑话

我们知道，笑话是小说的一种，属于街头巷尾的杂谈。威达雷通过《汉语口语初级读本》，向西方读者介绍了中国的寓言笑话。这些经作者改编自明清书面语的小故事，反映了中国人的思维方式，展示了中国式的幽默。

据笔者统计，威达雷从《笑林广记》等明清以来的几部笑话集中搜集语料，并将其转化成北京话。如《笑林广记·古艳部·启奏》的原文为：

> 一官被妻踏破纱帽。怒奏曰："臣启陛下，臣妻罗唣，昨日相争，踏破臣的纱帽。"上传旨云："卿须忍耐，皇后有些愈赖，与朕一言不合，平天冠打得粉碎。你的纱帽只算得个卵袋。"（游戏主人、程世爵）

此文被收入《汉语口语初级读本》时，题目未做改变，但表述的文字换作了20世纪初的北京话：

> 有一位老爷被太太踹碎了他的纱帽。心里很有气。就进宫奏事。说。臣启陛下。臣妻凶横。因为彼此拌嘴。将臣的纱帽打破。求皇上把他治罪。皇上就口传旨意。说。卿家。总得要忍耐些儿才是。你不知道正宫皇后。也有点儿愈赖。昨儿个与朕一言不合。将朕的平天冠。扯得粉碎。我朕还不敢生气哪。你那一顶纱帽。又算了甚么值钱的东西呢。（第7页）

从行文来看,不仅去掉了原文中的粗鄙用词,而且大大增加儿化等北京话特色。其实,威达雷除了从清游戏主人编《笑林广记》中选用素材外,也从明浮白斋主人《雅谑》、明冯梦龙《广笑府》、明赵南星《笑赞》、清石成金《笑得好》等其他几部明清笑话集中搜集了一些思想健康、文笔纯熟的篇目,只是他将文言改编成了当时的北京话。如《广笑府·一钱莫救》原文为:

一人性极鄙吝,道遇溪水新涨,吝出渡钱,乃拼命涉水。至中流,水急冲倒,漂流半里许。其子在岸旁觅舟救之。舟子索钱,一钱方往。子只出五分,断价良久不定,其父垂死之际,回头顾其子大呼曰:"我儿,我儿,五分便救,一钱莫救!"(冯梦龙)

该篇收到了《汉语口语初级读本》中,不仅题目改作"溺水",内容也做了改动:

有一个人。掉在水里了。他儿子大声嚷着说。快来救人哪。救上来。我必重重儿的谢候他。他父亲在水里。也探出头来。高声的喊叫。说要是三分银子。便来救我。若是要的多。教他们不必来救。(第113页)

可以说,改编后的文本,简洁易懂,口语色彩明显。《汉语口语初级读本》中的个别篇目如"训子",《广笑府》和《笑林广记》中均有收录,只是威达雷改编后的行文与两书不同,更加平易朴实,口语化的特色极为明显。

(二)书中保留了大量的北京话语料

《汉语口语初级读本》所收录的99篇笑话故事,采用了比较典型的北京官话来进行记录。

在语音方面,大量使用儿化韵,这是典型的北京话特征。然而其中也有个别故事记录了其他地区的方言读音。如第55个笑话"陕西诗"中,"绿念溜""疙念嘎""革落念嘎拉""红念浑"就记录了当时陕西方言的读音。

词汇方面,《汉语口语初级读本》使用了不少北京话词汇,如"长虫""煮饽饽""末了儿"(书中还收了"末末了、末后儿、到了儿"等同义词)、"起"(如"正在说话的工夫儿,就见太太起后堂猛然出来")、"滂""讨愧""伙""夠咸"等词。其中保留了部分文言词,如"堪堪"(渐渐、慢慢)。除此之外,书中还使用了一些同素逆序词。有的词形不同,意思差别较大,如"兄弟／弟兄",前者是指弟弟,后者是指兄长和弟弟二人;还有一些同素逆序词如"共总、耍戏、较比、嚏喷"等则与现代汉语中的通用形式(总共、戏耍、比较、喷嚏)意义相同或者相近。

语法方面,副词"狠"和"很"、语气词"了"和"咯"意义和用法完全相同,但均有较高的出现频率。至于当时为什么会出现这样的情形,尚需进一步研究。

(三) 符合汉语口语读本的基本要求

《汉语口语初级读本》句式简短,表意明确,生僻词语少,十分符合威达雷将其用作官话口语读本的要求。另外,其中的幽默风趣的语言,含蓄蕴藉的韵味,从输入的角度来说,有利于提高汉语学习者的兴趣。只不过其中内容与当时来华西方人的生活略有距离,对于学习者来说又有一定的影响。

威达雷在《汉语口语初级读本》中选用且改编了明清时期流行的寓言笑话,一方面为我们保留了当时北京话的语言面貌,另一方面有利于当时的西方人学习北京话,同时也向西方人推介了中国的文学样式,加深了他们对中国文化的了解。

参考文献

胡　适（1917）文学改良刍议，《新青年》第二卷第五号。

司德敷（Milton Theobald Stauffer）［美］等编（1922/1987）《中华归主——中国基督教事业统计（1901—1920）》，中国社会科学出版社，北京，1987。

图莉安（Antonella Tulli）［意大利］著，蔡雅菁译，许元真修编（2007）意大利汉学研究的历史（十九世纪之前），《文津流觞》第二十一期。

冯梦龙（明）《冯梦龙全集》第10集，凤凰出版社，南京，2007。

姚小平（2009）《罗马读书记》，外语教学与研究出版社，北京。

游戏主人、程世爵（清）《笑林广记二种》，齐鲁书社，济南，1996。

张美兰、陈思羽（2006）清末民初北京口语中的话题标记——以100多年前几部域外汉语教材为例，《世界汉语教学》第2期。

中国社会科学院近代史研究所翻译室（1981）《近代来华外国人名辞典》

《北京儿歌》导读

李海英

一、《北京儿歌》简介

《北京儿歌》初版于1896年，书中收录了170首在中国广泛流传的童谣，共220页，又名《北京童谣》《北京歌唱》《中国民间传说》。之所以出现四种中文译名，是因为该书封面的英文书名为*Pekinese Rhymes*，而扉页上又出现"Chinese folklore, first collected and edited with notes and translation"的英文字样。基于封面，其中文书名被译作《北京儿歌》或《北京童谣》《北京歌唱》；基于扉页，中文书名则被译作了《中国民间传说》。

二、《北京儿歌》的体例

《北京儿歌》由序言、索引和170首儿歌三部分构成。

第一部分为序言，用英文撰写，介绍威达雷搜集儿歌素材的各种甘苦以及儿歌内容带给他的感受。作者对这些作品表达了由衷的喜爱，他觉得虽然有一些词句较为简单，但非常感人，汉语水平不高的学习者也会从中感受到诗意。

第二部分是索引，内容包括170首儿歌的第一句及其页码。每句诗歌占一行，每一行从左向右横排，最左侧是每首儿歌第一句的威妥玛拼音，中间标出该句所在的页数，最右侧是这一句的中文。儿歌按照每句第一个音节首字母音序编排先后。比如，第一行是第九首儿歌的首句"张大嫂"，原因是"Chang[1]"的音序最靠前。

第三部分为170首儿歌。由中文原文、要点难点的英文注解、儿歌的英文翻译三个部分构成。

中文原文采用自左向右的横排方式，这是今天读者相对熟悉的排版方式，在当时算是一个不小的进步。因为当时印书要么采用从右向左的传统竖排方式，要么采用从左向右的横排印刷，而教会书籍往往采用后者。《北京儿歌》应该是在当时受了欧洲排版方式的影响，证据就是扉页上"Pei-T'ang Press"的字样。"北堂"就是当时北京遣使会印书馆的简称，它在当时是重要的天主教印刷机构（司德敷等 1987）。

要点难点的英文注解，采用了有话则长无话则短的做法。只要是作者感觉会构成阅读和理解障碍的，便会挑出做解释。解释的方法是先给出中文，接着是威妥玛拼音注音，最后是英文解释。若是遇到难懂的地方，威达雷会给出更多的背景介绍，有的甚至远远超出童谣中原有的词语。比如第47首童谣里的"铁拐李""西游记"，第48首中的"逛灯""灯节"等词，就没有出现在童谣中。有些背景知识的介绍，可以说是不厌其烦，如在解释"猴儿头"（北京方言指钱）一词的意思时，除了对北京话中类似的词语"大轱辘"和"官板"也做了介绍，还指出"古嘎""侧"和"侧罗"是与钱有关的临时用法。反过来，有些儿歌简单易学，作者就没有给出注解，如第146、147两首儿歌，就只有翻译而没有注解。

儿歌的英文翻译是与中文原文完全对应的，这对于母语不是汉语的学习者来说，有利于他们加深对汉语童谣的理解。当时汉语读本的编写者普遍采用的这种完全对译法，从对外汉语教学的角度来看，应该属于以奥伦多夫（Heinrich Gottfried Ollendorff）为代表的语法翻译法。

当然，《北京儿歌》有些英文注解和全文翻译跟中文原文有偏差。比如第156首儿歌中，英文注解将"大娘"和"二娘"解释为"大儿子二儿子的妻子"，但到了全文英译时就成了"同一个人的大房和二房"，前后出现了矛盾。另外第24首将"立秋"译为"the beginning of winter"，第147首中将"亲家太太"翻译为"a lady relation"，也有悖于汉语词语的原意。

三、《北京儿歌》的价值

（一）《北京儿歌》表现了作者威达雷对于中国民谣的重视

在第一版的序言里，威达雷详细介绍了寻找《北京儿歌》素材时的困难。一开始，作者根本不清楚该到哪里搜集童谣。当向中文老师求教时，"这个文化人认为这种通俗的东西属于垃圾，在中文中不存在"。在当时，民谣被国内读书人视为不登大雅之堂的东西。后来威达雷出了高价，这位中文教师才找到了四十首童谣。也许，恰恰因为是外国人，威达雷才能置身事外，不受当时中国国内否定民间文学、俗文学风气的羁绊。之所以这样说，是因为直到二十年后，新文化运动的代表人物胡适在倡导文学改革时对国内轻视民间歌谣的风气仍深有感触，他认为当时"还不曾晓得俗话里有许多可以供给我们取法的风格与方法，所以他们宁可学那不容易读又不容易懂的生硬的文句，却不屑研究那自然流利的民歌风格，这个似乎是今日诗国的一桩缺陷罢"（胡适1917）。

（二）作者从中发现了中国人与欧洲人尤其是意大利人在诗律方面的相似性

为了清楚地观察中国人生活的细节与背景，威达雷不遗余力地收集那些反映中国人生活的作品，童谣可以说是一个极好的切入点。这些童谣没有作者，它们或是出自哄孩子入睡的妈妈之手，或是由学校里的调皮男生不想上课时写成的。它们"如同野地里的花,自由自在地开放,无人知晓,也以同样的方式消失"。按照作者的说法,"应当引起大家注意的是其中的生动性,即使它们来自没有什么文化的人,对于书面语没有什么了解,但它们表现出同欧洲各国尤其是意大利诗歌一样的表达的生动性。(这么说的)理由在这些歌谣之上,在人民的真感情之上,(从这里)一种新的民族的诗也许能产生出来"。威达雷认为,即使对那些仅仅具备一点汉语表达手段的人来说,这些简单童谣也有动人之处,有真正的诗的火花。

(三)反映了19世纪末北京话的诸多特点

首先,在语音方面,《北京儿歌》真实地反映了北京话语音。如"伯"有三个读音puo^2,pai^1,pai^3;"饿不死"读作ngo^4 pu^4 ssu^3;"肉"读作jou^4。这些读音至今还保留在北方方言中。此外,该书一个很大的特点是保留了大量的儿化读音。

其次,《北京儿歌》记录了大量的北京话词汇。其中的名词如"押虎子"(北京街头的打更人)、"咕咕丢儿"(枣种儿)、"窝儿薄脆"(一种便宜点心)、"双棒儿"(孪生子)、"凉凉簪儿"(一种玻璃簪子)、"波棱盖儿"(膝盖)、"窝抠眼"(眼窝深陷)、"吉了儿/蛣蟟儿"(知了)、"肥瘦儿"(指好肉,有肥有瘦)、"闸草"(灯笼草);动词如"走筹"(巡逻)、"打提溜"(人或物因悬空挂起而晃动)、"耍叉"(打架)等;形容词有"利利拉拉、血丝胡拉、胖咕囤墩"等;拟声词则有"唏流哗啦、哇儿呱、嘚儿嗒"等。

除此之外,《北京儿歌》中也出现了部分少数民族词语,如"达子饽饽、阿煞、蚂虎子"等就来自满语。

在语法方面,《北京儿歌》在使用连锁式等拷贝式话题结构句上比较普遍。(如第58首:铁蚕豆,大把儿抓,娶了个媳妇就不要妈,要妈就要叉,要叉就分家。)而在清末民初,流行于日本、朝鲜的几部域外汉语教材则较少见到这种拷贝式话题结构句（张美兰、陈思羽2006）。这可能与《北京儿歌》的追求朗朗上口的语体特点有一定关系。从另一个侧面也说明，选用不同母语背景、不同语体的北京口语读本，有利于我们看到清末民初北京话语法的全貌。

（四）反映了19世纪末中国的社会现实和北京的民风民俗

在《北京儿歌》中，威达雷为读者展示了晚清中国社会生活的方方面面。如介绍了当时童谣经常采用"头子"（起兴）的习惯；涉及当时的风俗如下定、陪送、祭灶、灯节、喝杂银钱、轧腰儿等；表现的人物外形也有不同，有裹小脚儿的太太、戴困秋帽的爷爷、拿摩勒鱼儿的和尚。书中还表现了各个层面的人际关系，如中国的商业竞争、婆媳关系的复杂、姑嫂关系的尴尬等；反映了当时形形色色的观念，如对山西人的嘲笑、对回族人的歧视、对和尚的轻蔑、对婚后男子怕老婆的讽刺，以及重男轻女等思想。

就像威达雷在1896年9月30日所作的序言中总结的那样，《北京儿歌》的特点有三：

1. 其中的词汇和文字在他处几乎见不到；

2. 可以清楚地了解中国人生活的细节与背景；

3. 在通俗的歌谣中蕴含着真正的诗。

威达雷《北京儿歌》中的词汇和文字在他处见不到的看法，也并不符合事实。和威达雷同时或前后不久到达中国的西方人，编有好几部反映官话方言的民谣集。比如美国卫理公会传教士何德兰（Isaac Taylor Headland，1859—1942）所编写的《中国歌谣集》（又译作《孺子歌图》，*Chinese Mother Goose Rhymes*，1900）也采用中英文对照的形式写成，其中收集童谣150首，其体例为先用漂亮的汉字书法写出中文原文，然后翻译成英文，并且作者还为每首童谣配上了自己拍摄的儿童生活照片。其中不少童谣篇目与

《北京儿歌》相同或者相似，如两书都收录了下列这首："月亮爷／亮堂堂∥街坊的姑娘要嫁妆∥锭儿粉／棒儿香∥棉花胭脂二百张。"可以说，《中国歌谣集》和《北京儿歌》中的不少内容可以作为同一作品的不同版本比对来看。

意大利人威达雷以中国童谣的搜集和翻译作为切入点，既展现了东西方诗歌和儿童跨越国家和种族的共通性，又展示了晚清民风民俗，方便当时西方人了解中国。尤其是其中所采用的北京话，保留了清末民初北京话的语言面貌，对于今天的汉语教学和研究也是一座不可多得的宝库。

参考文献

胡　适（1917）文学改良刍议，《新青年》第二卷第五号。

司德敷（Milton Theobald Stauffer）［美］等编（1922/1987）《中华归主——中国基督教事业统计（1901—1920）》，中国社会科学出版社，北京，1987。

图莉安（Antonella Tulli）[意大利]著，蔡雅菁译，许元真修编（2007）意大利汉学研究的历史（十九世纪之前），《文津流觞》第二十一期。

冯梦龙（明）《冯梦龙全集》第10集，凤凰出版社，南京，2007。

姚小平（2009）《罗马读书记》，外语教学与研究出版社，北京。

游戏主人、程世爵（清）《笑林广记二种》，齐鲁书社，济南，1996。

张美兰、陈思羽（2006）清末民初北京口语中的话题标记——以100多年前几部域外汉语教材为例，《世界汉语教学》第2期。

中国社会科学院近代史研究所翻译室（1981）《近代来华外国人名辞典》

A FIRST READING BOOK FOR STUDENTS
OF COLLOQUIAL CHINESE

CHINESE MERRY TALES

COLLECTED AND EDITED

BY

BARON GUIDO VITALE

Chinese Secretary to the Italian Legation.

PEKING

PEI-T'ANG PRESS

1901

TO

THE STUDENTS OF CHINESE

PREFACE

In 1896 I began to collect odd scraps of Chinese Folklore and published my Pekingese Rhymes.

The ninety nine tales contained in this book and written down in mandarin dialect belong doubtlessly to the folklore.

However, the natural aversion that every Chinaman able to write and read entertains against the colloquial, led to the fact that these tales which are so commonly known and quoted, are to be found in literary style only.

I brought these, which I have chosen among thousands, into mandarin and I hope that the Student of colloquial Chinese may derive some benefit from a reading book so easily divided into many daily lessons and bringing some element of mirth into the sad and dreary task of learning Chinese.

BARON G. A. VITALE.

Peking the 31 July 1901.

INDEX

		Pag.
1.	Vine-bowers and their dangers	1
2.	A selfsacrifying neighbour	2
3.	The easiest way to learn chinese	3
4.	How useful may be the biggest volumes of learning	4
5.	Where do you go?	5
6.	Imperial griefs	7
7.	The grateful debtor	7
8.	Tea or a bath?	9
9.	The tamed magistrate	10
10.	Scepticism and cruelty of cats	10
11.	Easy way of removing	11
12.	The man who is "more right"	12
13.	"I burned him yesterday"	12
14.	Asking the road	15
15.	The happiness of blind men	16
16.	The thirsty dog	17
17.	The hen-pecked hussbands club	18
18.	Disputing about etiquette	19
19.	Unlucky words for a student	20
20.	The griefs of a literary husband	21
21.	Explaining the classics	22
22.	The dog as a teacher	23
23.	Where do I go?	25
24.	Military examinations	26
25.	The golden ox	27
26.	Gratefulness of a target God	28
27.	Harmful vengeance	29
28.	His wife's true age	30
29.	Hiding the spade	32

		pag.
30.	Your head is too soft	33
31.	The portrait-painter	34
32.	The hardships of a tailor	33
33.	Reckoning the age	35
34.	The rope and the ox	37
35.	Sorry remembrance	38
36.	About bridges in Soochow and turnips in Shantung	39
37.	Ingenious talking	40
38.	Kick please!	41
39.	Jealousy in dreams	42
40.	The shamed thief	43
41.	The deaf and the dumb	44
42.	The way of paying half-price	45
43.	Take a chair!	46
44.	The likeness of a portrait	48
45.	The charm against mosquitoes	49
46.	One pair of shoes for two	50
47.	She is thinking of the boatman	51
48.	The drum of wonder	52
49.	Hypocrisy of religious persons and cats	43
50.	The hasty man	54
51.	Riding a tiger	55
52.	Attractions of music	56
53.	Hardships of travelling	57
54.	The griefs of a tiger	59
55.	Shan-hsi poetry	60
56.	How books may be useful	61
57.	Sparing half-glass	62
58.	Very good fists!	63

pag.

59.	Difference of taste	64
60.	The Taoist Priest on the door	65
61.	Differences in relationship	66
62.	This humble moon	67
63.	The ascetic cat	68
64.	How rare are the great sages	69
65.	Riches of a beggar	70
66.	Prayers and domestic economy	71
67.	A shoemaker in hell	72
68.	Difference in punctuation	74
69.	How to save a father	76
70.	Bad luck of a doctor	77
71.	The charitable deceiver	78
72.	Brotherly cultivation of fields	80
73.	The refrain of the song	81
74.	The square serpent	82
75.	The salt eggs	83
76.	Two taels a night	83
77.	The way of going to hell	86
78.	How to pay debts	87
79.	The theft of wine	90
80.	The one thousand taels	93
81.	Conversational misunderstandings	94
82.	The price of shoes	95
83.	The ranks of nobility	97
84.	Tall monkeys	98
85.	Rich and poor	99
86.	The boasters	99
87.	The voyage to Soochow	103
88.	The two pair of shoes	104

		pag.
89.	Wrong writing	104
90.	The big mosquitoes	106
91.	The brothers liars	107
92.	Talking of the sky	109
93.	Dead by mistake	110
94.	Kill me by half	111
95.	How to heal a hunchbak	112
96.	Economy in danger	113
97.	Only I and a beggar	114
98.	The great washing-tub	116
99.	The arrow wound	117

第一 倒葡萄架

有一位知縣坐堂審案。書班上堂來伺候。滿臉的傷痕。就問他。你臉上怎麼咯。他說昨兒晚上。在葡萄架底下涼快來着。忽然颳了一陣風。把葡萄架颳躺下了。故此受了傷了。那個官不信。說你這明明是指甲抓的傷。必是和你女人打架來着。被他抓傷的。是不是。那個書班臉一紅。說老爺猜的不錯。老爺說你女人怎麼這麼利害。等我把他傳了來。打他一頓。給你出出氣。正在說話的工夫兒。就見太太起後堂猛然出來。說。你要打誰。老爺忙着就和官人們說。咱們退堂。你們快散罷。老爺的葡萄架。眼看着也要躺下了。

第二 借牛

有個鄉下人。給本村的財主寫了一個字兒來。要借一頭牛。恰巧這位財主正同着客人吃飯。這個財主雖然有錢。原來他不認得字又不好請客人替他念念。他就拿起這個字兒。假裝着看了一遍。就對着來人兒說這件事好辦。

第三訓子

有一個有錢的老頭子。不認得字。別人勸他請了一位先生。好教訓他兒子。這個學生先學一字兒。就畫了一畫。二字。畫了兩畫。三字。畫了三畫。學生把筆擱下了。就告訴他父親說。這個字義兒。孩兒都明白了。要一位先生幹甚麼呢。他父親聽他說這個話。心裏狠樂。可就把先生辭了。這一天。他父親要請一位姓萬的朋友吃飯。叫他兒子一早

你先囬去罷。等一會兒。我自己就走了去咯。

寫個請帖。到了晌午。還沒有寫完哪。他父親就到了書房問他。說這麼幾個字。也值得這麼費事。他兒子撅着嘴就和他父親說。甚麼姓的朋友您交不得。您偏要交這麼一個姓萬的。您瞧。從早起我寫到這個時候兒咯。我纔寫了五百畫。那兒就寫彀了一萬的數兒哪。

第四 書低

有個書生。在和尙廟裏讀書。頭一天早起出去遊玩去了。午後進房。就叫書童兒拿書來。書童就拿了一本文選來。

書生說低。童兒又擎了一本漢書來。他仍舊嘆低。又拿了一本史記來。他還說是低。因為他的屋子和和尚聽他說這個話。就狠詫異。過來就問這位書生說。這三樣兒書要是念熟了一本。可以稱個飽學。閣下怎麼還說是低。這是甚麼緣故呢。書生說。我原要睡覺。為的是拿書落起來。高高兒的。好當個枕頭。

第五　何往

有一個人天生的獸傻。不懂的文墨。在道兒上遇見一個斯文的朋友。說兄何往。這個獸子一聽他問。他是分毫不懂。不能答言兒。他可就把何往倆字記住咯。又請教別人。別的人都知道他是個獸子。就耍戲他。說何往兩個字是一句罵人的話兒。他聽見就有了氣了。告訴他這句話的人分了手就走了。到了第二天。又遇見那個朋友咯。還是問着他說兄何往。這個獸子就氣恨恨的說。我是不何往。你到要何往。

第六啓奏

有一位老爺被太太踹碎了他的紗帽。心裏很有氣。就進宮奏事說。臣啓陛下。臣妻凶橫。因爲彼此拌嘴將臣的紗帽打破。求皇上把他治罪。皇上就口傳旨意說。卿家。總得要忍耐些兒纔是。你不知道正宮皇后。也有點兒憊賴昨兒個與朕一言不合。將朕的平天冠扯得粉碎。我朕還不敢生氣哪。你那一項紗帽又算了甚麽值錢的東西呢。

第七扛欠戶

有個該錢的人。賬主兒屢次的和他要。他就是不還。那個放賬的人。就氣極了。告訴他的底下人說。你們在他的門口兒。偷偷兒的等着。他那一時出來。你們把他給我扛了來我和他要。他不還我不放他走。底下人就天天兒去。在他門口兒鷩着。這一天。他剛一出門兒。派下人就把他弄躺下了。扛起來就走。走了半天底下人乏了說。倸們找個地方兒歇歇兒。那個該錢的在肩髈兒上說。快走罷。別跕住腳倘若歇着又教別的賬主兒。把我扛了去咯。那可不干我的事。

第八 留茶

有客人前來看望。主人總得沏茶欵待。有一天有客來了。主人家一點兒茶葉沒有。就叫小童兒往街坊家借去。去了半天。總沒有囘來。這鍋裏的水是遂開遂添趕到工夫兒大了。水也添滿了。這個茶葉到了兒還是沒借了來。他們太太兒。就把他的男人請進來。告訴他說。客人的茶。我看着是喝不成了。莫若你留下他。請他洗個澡罷。

第九 知縣怕婆

有一位知縣。專怕太太。這一天正在坐堂。忽然聽見科房裏吵嚷。叫皂隸去看看是甚麼事。皂隸回來了。說回老爺的話。是兵房裏的書班。他們兩口子打架哪。知縣聽見說。就咬牙大怒。說若是我我。我誰知太太兒在後堂聽見。就出來。大聲兒嚷着說若是你便怎麼樣。知縣笑着說。是我。他就勢兒給太太兒跪下了。要是我如何下得手去打呢。

第十 貓逐鼠

有個貓專會拏耗子。這一天把一個耗子追進瓶裏去了。

就捨不得走。在瓶的旁邊兒悄悄兒的蹲着等他出來。耗子是真怕的利害。不敢出頭。那個貓忽然就打了一個噴嚏。耗子在瓶裏就說了一句吉祥話兒。說您大吉大利貓說不相干。任憑你怎麼奉承我好。我還是要吃你。

第十一 求人搬家

有一個人最好清靜。他所住的屋子是在銅匠鐵匠的房子兩夾間兒。每天這兩個人做活。吵的他不得個安生。他可就常對着這兩個人說。若是你們二位有信搬家。可先告訴我一聲。我好好兒的預備個東兒。請請二位。這一天。兩個匠人都過來了。說。我們兩下裏要搬家咯。先通知您哪。您不是許下要請我們麼。故此特來叨擾。這個人聽這個話樂極了。趕緊的叫了一棹酒席。請他們倆吃喝。趕到吃喝完了。就問說。你們二位要搬在甚麼地方兒去呀。那兩個人就說了。他是要搬在他屋裏。我要搬在他屋裏。

第十二 有理

有一位官。最愛貪贓。若要問案。頭幾天。先叫傳原告被告對審。這一天有倆打官司的。原告先送了五十兩銀子。被告兒聽見說。就加倍的送了一百兩銀子。到了審的那一天。那個官不問情由。就抽籤要打原告。那原告兒打着手勢兒。比作五個數兒。說小的是有理的。那個官說。奴才你說你有理麽。就打着手勢兒。一翻一覆的。比作了一百的數兒。給原告兒瞧。說他比你還更有理哪。

第十三 問令尊

有一個人要出外。就囑咐他兒子說。我走之後。要是有人來問你令尊。你可對他說。我的家父出外去了。請進來吃茶。他父親因為他兒子獃傻。恐怕他又忘了。就把這幾句話寫在紙上交給他。他兒子就把這個字兒裝在袖口兒裏頭咯。要用的時候兒。偷偷兒的拿出來再看過了三天。沒人來問。他兒子說。這個字兒沒用處了。這天晚上。在燈底下就燒了。趕到了第四天。忽然有客人來了。問他說。你的令尊呢。他在袖口兒裏掏了半天。找不着。就對着客人說沒了。客人聽他這個話。狠詫異。說多咱沒的。他兒子說。

昨兒晚上。敎我燒了。

第十四 問路

有一個近視眼的人。迷了路了看見道傍邊兒石頭樁子上落着個老鵄。他瞅着就疑惑是個人。他就望着他再三的問道兒。忽然那個老鵄飛起去了。那個近視眼的有了氣了。就朝着那個石頭樁子說。我問了你半天。你總不答應。你的帽子被風颳了去了。我也不告訴你。

第十五 被打

有兩個瞎子。在一塊兒走着說。世界上的人惟有俺們沒眼兒的最好。那有眼的天天兒奔忙。到了莊家人更利害。如何能像俺們清閒逍遙自在的哪。那莊家人聽他們倆自誇。就很有氣。暗暗兒的就湊了幾個人。假裝着縣太爺走路。就吆喝着說。這倆瞎子不知規矩。爲甚麼不廻避裝知縣的就說了。給我打。那些個人把瞎子按在地下。就用鋤把子打了一頓。打完了。喝叫滾罷。那倆瞎子趴起來就跑了。這個莊家漢跟在瞎子的後頭。偷着聽他們倆說甚麼。這個瞎子就和那個說。到了兒還是偺們沒眼兒好。要是個有眼兒的冲了知縣的執事不但打了一頓還要問個發罪呢。

第十六 犬症

有一個聾子上朋友家去看望。到了門口兒叫門那狗在外頭是不住聲兒的咬。這個工夫兒。可巧下起雨來了。他朋友給他開開了街門。就望裏讓。他就和朋友說。您那個尊犬。別是犯了水飲的症候了罷。現在乾渴的利害。您哪不信賬賬。他竟張着嘴。在那兒等着接雨水喝呢。

第十七 正夫綱

有許多懼內的。都因爲在家裏受各自各兒女人的打罵。這一天可巧都遇在一塊兒了。大家夥兒一商量找了個廟。說偺們整十個人。今兒偺們在佛爺跟前燒個香兒。拜一個把兄弟痛痛快快的吃喝一天。各自回家。再去受氣。商量明白了。就打酒買菜。預備得了正在吃喝高興的時候兒。想不到這十位太太兒。是不約而同。找在廟裏來不依那哥兒九個。都去找個地方兒藏躲偷看。就剩了一個人兒。在那兒坐着。巋然不動。任意兒教衆女人們吵鬧。他也不理。女人們嚷了半天。也就散了。這幾個人說。俗們沒有他膽子大。就讓他作個大盟兒罷。敢到過去一看說了不得了。俗們大爺早嚇的沒了氣兒坐化了。

第十八 爭座位

有一天瞎子矮子羅鍋子三個人。因爲喝酒都爭那一個上座兒。三個人說。俗們這麼着。誰能說一句大話。就讓他在上首裏座第一位。好不好。瞎子說。我的目中無人。該我坐矮子說。我非平常人可比。還是得讓我。羅鍋子說。你們倆別爭了。你們都是直背(姪輩)自然還是該我上坐。

第十九 及第

一位秀才上京鄉試去。他的底下人挑着行李。在後頭跟隨。走到曠野的地方兒。忽然颳了一陣大風。把行李上浮擱的帽子颳在地下了。底下人就大嚷着說。帽子落了地了。他主人聽他說這個話。很不喜歡。嫌喪氣。就囑咐他。說以後別說落地。總說及第。底下人說。喳。遵老爺的命。他就把帽子結結實實的綑在行李上。說。老爺偺們走罷。如今憑您就是走上天去。再也不能及第咯。

第二十 腹內無文

又有一個秀才。因考試的日子臨近咯。日夜憂愁。無精打彩。他媳婦看見他這個樣兒難受。就笑着和他說。我瞧你們作文章。怎麽這麽費事。彷彿我們娘兒們。養孩子一個樣兒的難。那個秀才就說。還是你們養孩子容易得很。他

第二十一 中酒

有位先生。在學館裏教書。這一天。學生就請教老師。問大學之道這句書。是怎麼講。先生不懂。立刻就裝着醉說。你們偏揀我喝多了的時候兒問我。我如何講的清楚呢。趕到放了學。先生囘家。就把學生請教的事。告訴了夫人兒媳婦問。怎麼見得。秀才說。你們肚子裏。有的是現成兒的。我的文才。是沒在肚子裏頭。怎麼不敎我為難。

一遍。他媳婦兒就說。大學是書的名兒。之道是書中的道理。這有甚麼難講的呢。到了第二天上了學。先生就和徒弟們說。你們實在無知。昨兒我喝醉了。偏來問我。今兒我醒着。又不來問。是甚麼緣故。你們昨兒所問的大學之道那一句。聽我講給你們聽。大學是書的名兒。之道就是書中的道理。你們明白咯沒有。學生說明白了。可就又問說下一句在明明德。是怎麼講呢。先生聽這一問。就倆眼七斜。說。且住。別忙。我的酒管保是又上來了。

第二十二 狗坐館

有一個人慣會說謊話。這一天對他親家說。舍下有三丈長的一隻牛。一天能走一千里。還有一隻報更雞。每逢交幾更。他就叫喚幾聲。又有一個狗。專能讀書識字。他的親家就很羨慕說府上有這樣兒的活寶。來日我必要到府上去瞻仰瞻仰。這個人就囘了家。對他媳婦說。怎麼好。貝顧我一時撒了謊。明兒親家來了。教我怎麼囘覆他。他媳婦兒說不要緊。明兒你走你的。我自有法子囘覆他。第二天他們親家果然來了。說親家在家麼。他媳婦說。您親家今兒一早騎牛上了雲南了。過幾天就囘來。親家說。府上還有一隻報更雞哪。正說話這個功夫兒。恰巧是晌午。那個雞就打起鳴兒來了。他媳婦兒指着這隻雞說。就是他。不但報時晨。要有生眼兒的人來。他還報呢。親家又問。讀書那個狗。拉出來賞我看看。他媳婦說。不瞞親家說。貝爲家寒。我敎他出外坐館敎書去了。

第二十三　我何在

有位典史。押解一個犯重罪的和尙。上省候審。在半道兒上。典史喝得爛醉如泥。人事不知。和尚偷偷兒的。把刑具扭壞。把鎖練子套在典史的脖子上。又拏小刀子把典史的頭髮都給他剃淨了。趕緊的逃跑了。到了第二天早起。典史的酒也醒了。和尚看不見了。摸了摸自己禿葫蘆。又看見脖子上帶着鐵練子。自己各兒納悶。哼。說和尚可是有了。我哪。我可往那兒去了。

第二十四 武弁夜巡

有一個武官查夜。拏住一個犯夜的。他自己稱爲學生。說我在朋友家作文會來着散的很晚。回家也就遲了。那個武官說。你旣是位書生等我考你一考。那學生說可以。請閣下出個題目。我好獻醜。那武官想了半天。想不起甚麼來說去罷。今兒便宜你。沒有題目。

第二十五 屬牛

有一位知縣。這一天是他的壽誕之期。闔衙門書班皁役。打聽老爺的屬相。是子年生人屬鼠兒的。大家夥兒。前幾天就湊錢打了一個赤金的耗子作爲壽禮。那位老爺看見大樂。說你們眾人的心思。實在用的巧妙。可是你們知道啊。太太的好日子也快到了。就剩了幾天兒咯。書役們說不曉得請示老爺。太太是某年生人。是甚麼屬相。老爺說。太太比我小一歲。他是個屬牛的。

第二十六垜子神助陣

有個帶兵的武官。這天和敵人打仗身臨陣前堪堪的要敗了。忽然有人前來助陣。反倒得了個勝仗。這武官就磕頭拜謝。說您是那位尊神前來救命。那神道說。我是垜子神。特來救你。武官說。下官待您有甚麼好處。敢勞尊神搭救。那垛子神就說。我感念你素日射箭的好處。從來沒有傷過我一箭。

第二十七 老父

有一個買賣人。因他兒子作了官。受了誥封咯。去拜會本地的知縣。縣官因他歲數兒大。就稱呼他個老先。他聽着氣忿忿的就回家來咯。他兒子問甚麼緣故。父親帶氣而回。他說這個知縣。欺我太甚。他應當稱呼我個老先生。繞是。他故意兒的作歇後語。叫我個老先明露着是藐視我的意思。我也同稱他來着。也沒教他得了便宜去。他兒子就問。您怎麼稱呼得他。他父親說。我應當稱呼他老父母纔是。我也把後頭那個字歇住了。我就叫了他一聲老父。

第二十八 瞞歲數

有個人娶了個老媳婦兒。乍一見面兒。看他臉上縐紋兒太多。可就問他。你有多大年紀咯。他媳婦兒說。我還小哪。纔四十五。他男人說。爲甚麼年庚帖兒上。寫着三十八哪。

據我看你。還不止於四十五歲。你得給我說實話。那媳婦說。我實在是五十四了。他男人還是不信。來囘的盤問。再也不肯說了。到了晚上。他男人想了個好法子。就告訴他媳婦兒說。你先睡覺罷我得看着我的鹽缸。昨兒教耗子偷吃了好些個。他媳婦兒聽見這個話。不由的哈哈的大笑。說老太太今年活了六十八咯。沒聽見人說過耗子會偷鹽吃。

第二十九 藏鋤

有一個莊家漢在地裏耕地。他女人叫他回家吃飯去。他就大聲兒的嚷着說。等我把鋤藏好了再去呀。趕他到了家。他女人就和他說。藏鋤本是嚴密的事兒。你這麼大呼小叫的豈不教人聽見偷了去嗎。你快去瞧瞧去罷。他回去一看罷咧。那把鋤早沒了。他就忙忙的跑回家裏。湊到他女人耳根子底下。悄不聲兒的說。那把鋤。已經教人偷了去咯。

第三十 頭嫩

有個剃頭的。這天給一個年輕的人剃頭。繞一下刀子就剌了個口子。還沒有剃完。就剌了好些個口子。剃頭的停住手。就推辭了。說我不給您剃咯。主人說。這是甚麼緣故。剃頭的說。您這個頭皮兒太嫩。不好剃。等您上了年紀。歲數兒也有了。頭皮兒也老梆咯。到那個時候兒。我再給您剃罷。

第三十一 寫真

有一個畫喜容兒的畫匠。在家裏閒住。竟等着人來請他。

可總沒個上門的買賣。別人就給他出了個主意。說把你們兩口兒的本模樣兒。畫成一幅行樂圖。掛在門口兒。就有人來請來咯。這個畫匠。就依計而行。可巧這天。他丈人來賒他們來咯。就問他女婿說門口兒掛着那個小娘兒們是誰。他女婿說。那就是您的令愛呀。您怎麼不認得他。他丈人說。旣然是我們姑奶奶。怎麼和一個面生的小夥子。並肩而坐。這是個甚麼樣子。

第三十二 不下剪

有一個裁縫。給人家裁衣裳。打算着要賺他幾尺布。拏着這疋布。來回的擺弄。攢眉縐目的。左右的爲難。這個空兒。可就不小了。總不肯下剪子。徒弟在傍邊兒。瞅着都着急了。就問他們掌櫃的說。師傅。這是怎麼咯。這麼爲難。裁縫就告訴徒弟說。有了我的。沒有他的。要是有了他的。可就沒有我的了。

第三十三 較歲數

有個姓張的。跟前有個姑娘繞一歲。又有個姓李的。跟前有個兩歲的小子。他就託人說這個姓張的姑娘。給他兒子作媳婦兒。這個姓張的聽見說。就很有氣。說他這不是欺負我嗎。我們姑娘今年纔一歲。他的兒子到兩歲咯。若是我們姑娘到了十歲。他的兒子已經是二十咯。我如何肯給這麼個老女婿哪。他們太太兒就和男人說。你算錯了。咱們姑娘。今年雖然一歲。等到明年。可就和他的兒子同歲咯。爲甚麼不給呢。

第三十四 盜牛

有一個扛枷的。親友遇見他。就問他說。你犯了甚麼罪咯。就至於這個樣子。這個人說。我偶然打街上走。見地下有根草繩兒。以為是沒甚麼用處。我就撿起來。挈着走咯。可就出了包了。他的親友說。就是惧撿這麼根草繩兒。何至於犯這麼大罪。這扛枷的說。你們不知道。這根繩兒上還拴着點兒東西。別人就問他。是甚麼東西呀。他說。還有一隻小小的耕牛。

第三十五 吞盃

有一個人好喝大酒。這天往一個朋友家去赴席。看見桌子上。這個酒盅子太小。他就故意兒的。作出要哭的樣子來。他的朋友看見吃了一驚。就問他說。這是甚麼緣故。這個人說。我今兒是覩物傷情。想起我們老人家去世的那一天。甚麼病兒都沒有。也是因為朋友請了去喝酒。那個酒盅。就像府上的是一個樣。先父連酒盅兒都攔在嘴裏沒嚥下去。教他給噎死了。我今兒在府上。又看見這個樣兒的酒盅兒。我爲得不哭。

第三十六 兩羨慕

有個山東人聽說蘇州的橋。又高又大。他也不怕道兒遠。一定要去看看。走到半道兒。可巧遇見一個蘇州人。這個蘇州人。原是聽見山東的蘿蔔最大。一心要往山東去看看蘿蔔。故此二人路遇。各道羨慕的意思。蘇州人就先說了。兄台不用去咯。遠路風塵的。等我說說這個橋的樣式就得了。說去年六月初三。這一天有個人由橋上掉下去咯。直到今年六月初三。還沒落到水皮兒上哪。您想這個橋。高大不高大。山東人就說了。多蒙您指敎。閣下不是要看敞處的蘿蔔嗎。我想您也就不必去咯。等到明年這個時候兒。那個蘿蔔長的自然也就到了你們蘇州了。

第三十七 活動話

有一個作父親的敎導兒子。說凡人說話。總要活動不可把話說死了。他兒子就問他父親怎麼叫活動話。他父就敎給他說我告訴你。比方街坊和你借東西。要看他是借甚麼咯。不可竟說多有。也不可竟說少有。也有家裏有的。

也有家裏沒有的。這就敎作活動話。你可記住。別忘了。這一天有客來拜。問他兒子說令尊在家沒有。他兒子可就用活動話。囘答那個朋友。說您問我父親哪。我也不好說多。我也不好說少。也有在家的。也有不在家的。

第三十八 願脚踢

有個打柴的樵夫。走在半道兒上。愰心中挈扁擔。把大夫碰了一下兒。大夫就用拳頭。要打他。那個樵夫跪在地下哀告。說老爺您千萬別動手。挈脚踢我幾下子罷。傍邊看熱鬧兒的人都詫異。說這是甚麼緣故。樵夫說衆位不知道。這位是大夫。他要用腳踢我幾下兒我未必就死。他納要是一上手。我一定就活不成了。

第三十九 吃夢中醋

有一個怕媳婦兒的人。這天在睡夢中。忽然大笑。他女人把他搖醒了。說你夢見甚麼得意的事咯。這麼樂。他男人不敢撒謊。說我夢中納一美妾。故此我樂極了。他女人聽說就氣極了。叫他先跪在床下。找家法要打他。他男人就說。這作夢本是虛假。你如何當成眞事。他女人說。別的夢都許你作。像這個樣兒的夢後來不准你作。男人說以後不作就是咯。他女人說我不信。你睡着了作夢。你自各兒知道。我那兒能知道呢。他男人就說。我從今兒起一年三百六十天。夜夜兒醒到天亮。再也不敢睡覺就是了。

第四十 羞見賊

有一個賊。往窮人家裏去偷東西。進了屋門看見主人的臉兒朝外睡覺哪。見他進來。忽然翻了個身。臉兒又朝裏去咯。這個賊心裏就疑惑着說。別是熟人罷。看見我怕我害羞他就望外溜着要跑。只見那個主人大嚷着說來來不妨不妨。我是因爲家寒。無物可敬實在是沒臉見您哪。

第四十一譁聾啞

有一個聾子和一個啞吧兩個人。各自遮掩各自的毛病。這天聾子遇見啞吧。求他唱個曲兒那個啞吧。明明兒知道他是個聾子。就用嘴唇兒。一張一合的還用手拍打着。作出唱的個樣子來。這個聾子也就故意兒的側耳聞聽。

見那啞吧的嘴唇子不住的動彈。就大聲兒嚷着說。好極了。好極了。總沒聽見閣下唱了。今兒一聽。比頭裏唱的強多了。

第四十二 取金

有一位知縣。出了一張硃票。要用兩錠赤金。那鋪子見票。趕緊的送了來。當堂領那個買金子的價值。官就問他價值多少。鋪子的人說。平價該當領若干。如今既是老爺用。就領個半價罷。這位老爺。就望兩邊兒的官人說。既是這麼樣。發一錠還他就是了。發了金子之後鋪子的人還是等着領價。老爺說。價值已經給了。怎麼還要鋪子人說。老爺多偺給了。老爺聽這個話。不由的大怒。說刁奴才。你說就領半價。故此還你一錠。足抵了你一半的價值。本縣並不虧負你。你怎麼這麼糊塗。快給我把他攆出去。

第四十三 坐椅子

有一家兒要賬的人太多。椅子板凳都坐滿了。還有一個在門磴兒上坐着的。主人就偷偷兒告訴他說。請閣下明兒個早些兒來。那個要賬的會意兒。這必是明兒早起。主人先還我的欠賬。心裏很喜歡。可就嚷着說。主人實在沒錢。俗們大家夥兒散了罷。趕到第二天一黑早。他就先去了。請主人出來還錢。那主人見了他。說不是我要還錢因爲閣下昨兒在門礎兒上坐着我心裏不安。故此請閣下今兒早些兒來。先佔下一把椅子坐着省的衆人都來了。閣下又沒有坐位兒咯。

第四十四鬍鬚像

有一個畫喜容兒的。給人畫完了。就和主人說。我幫您擎着您的尊容。伱們沿着道兒問人家看看我畫的像不像。主人說很好。就這麽辦。剛一出門兒。可巧遇見一個人。主人就說勞您駕。請您看看像我不像那個人對准了主人看了半天。說這頂帽子畫的倒像。後來又遇見了一個人。主人又說再請您看看像我不像那個人說衣裳畫的很像。到了第三個人咯。畫畫兒的。沒等主人問他先說了。帽子衣裳都有人說過了。不勞再說了。就問臉面兒看看畫的像不像。那個人看完了尋思了半天。說鬍鬚畫的最像。

第四十五 驅蚊

有一個老道。自誇說我專會畫符驅蚊。決不敢飛來咬人。就有一位再三的求他。說我屋裏蚊子最多。咬的我整夜不能合眼。您把符賞給我一道。我得着覺睡。我就感恩不盡了。老道就畫了一道。叫他拏囘去貼上管保靈驗。到了這天晚上。屋裏的蚊子更多。還是一夜沒睡。這個人就找老道不依去咯。老道說我不信。看你貼在那兒了。那個人說我貼在牆上了。老道說那就怨不得了。你貼的不得法。那個人說怎麼纔得法呢。老道說你把蚊子都哄淨了。放下蚊帳來。把我的符貼在蚊帳裏頭。自然就沒有蚊子咯。

第四十六夥穿靴

有親哥兒倆湊錢。夥買了一雙靴子。哥哥白日裏穿着。天兒出門。不是拜客。就是赴席。兄弟心裏不願意抱委曲。他就想了個主意好撈本兒。夜夜兒他把靴子穿上。在院子裏來囘的整走這麼一夜。過了幾天。靴子也走破了。穿不得了。哥哥又敎兄弟攤錢。說咱們倆再買一雙罷。兄弟說。您一個人兒買罷。我也不穿了。我可得睡覺咯。

第四十七 想船家

有一位敎書的先生放了節學。在家裏閒住。這天他女人打了個嚏噴。他就說。准是有人在背地裏講究我哪。先生說。我在學房也是常常兒的打嚏噴。他女人說。那是我想你哪。趕到過了節。先生仍然去上學舘。可就辭別他女人。

上了船了。忽然船家被風吹了鼻子。連打了幾個噴嚏。那先生就蹉着脚兒說。不好了。我剛纔出了門兒。我女人就在家裏想着船家了。

第四十八謊鼓

有一個人好說大離話。說做處廟裏。有一個大鼓。大有幾十圍。要是打一下兒。那個聲音能聽一百多里地。傍邊兒有個駁文兒的人說了。我們本處有一隻牛頭在江南。尾巴在江北。有幾萬觔那麽重。豈不是件奇事。衆人不信這個人就說了。若沒有我們那兒那麼大的牛。怎麼能得這張大皮去幪他那面大鼓呢。

第四十九 心狠

有一個淘氣的孩子。把念經的誦珠兒給貓掛在脖子上了。衆耗子瞧見了。就彼此的道喜說貓大老爺現在掛珠兒好佛動了慈悲善念咯。一定就不吃偺們了。大家夥兒這麼一樂。都出來在滿地下鬧着頑兒。貓看見了。一連就撲了好幾個。衆耗子嚇的就各處兒藏躱。都在背地裏抱怨着說。我當是他老人家。眞是改惡從善。發了慈心了。原來是假意修行的。又有個耗子說。你不知道。如今世上那修行念佛的心腸兒更狠十倍。

第五十作揖

有兩位親家。一個性急。一個性慢。這天在道兒上遇見了。這個慢性兒親家。就給那個急性子的親家。一恭到地說。正月逛燈擾元宵。五月節又賞粽子。八月中秋。又送我月餅菓子。這麽屢次的叨擾。我還沒有囘敬哪。實在是討愧的很。他交代完了這套話。這繞直起腰來。誰知道性急的親家嫌煩。早躲開了。慢性兒的親家。一瞧沒有人了。就問別人說我們舍親是甚麼時候兒走的。那旁邊兒人說就打你們逛燈之後。他就走了已經走了多半天咯。

第五十一　騎虎

有一個人走山路遇見一隻老虎。他就爬上樹去。那個老虎在樹底下躦進要上去吃他。他一害怕打樹上掉下來了。可巧正掉在老虎的脊梁背兒上。沒法子。他就騎上摟着老虎的腰。由着老虎的性兒走罷。傍邊兒的人看見了。不知底裏。可就和別人說。你瞧這個人騎着個老虎。他在上頭坐着。就像個神仙。有多麼自在。這個人聽見了。在虎的身上就太嚷着說。你們瞧着我有多大的威風似的。那兒知道我心裏。要下去下不去。問不得我怎麼難受咯。

第五十二 市中彈琴

有一位彈琴的先生。在熱鬧街兒上彈琴。本處的人。都當是他彈的必是絃子琵琶那些東西。聽的人不少。後來聽他彈的那個聲兒清淡。一點兒不熱鬧。都不愛聽可就慢慢兒的都散了。末末了兒。就剩下一個人咯。站着不動。這個彈琴的先生說好了。這纔是我個知音的人哪。也不枉我彈了這麼半天。這個人說。我也是不懂。我不走。就因為這張棹子。是我們家的。我竟等着你彈完了。我好扛了家去。要不是這麼着。我早走了多半天了。

第五十三　出外好

有一個客人。僱了一隻船上杭州去。就使喚船上的人。這天清早起來。打米煮飯。船上的稍婆。背着客人把淘過的濕米。偸着撈起一大碗來藏在竈火坑裏。可巧敎客人看見了。又不好明說出來。坐在艙裏頭。不住的嚷着說。在家千日難。出外一時好。稍婆聽見了。說客人你說錯了。我知道是在家千日好。出外一時難。這兩句話。爲甚麼客人說顚倒了呢。客人可就說了。你旣知道我難。求你把竈火坑裏的那一大碗米給我下在鍋裏。就不難咯。

第五十四 虎訴苦

有一個和尚。挾着一卷經。拿着一副鏡。上村兒裏去作佛事。走到半道兒。忽然遇見一個老虎。冲着他撲了來咯。嚇的和尚沒法子。他就拿那副鏡對准了老虎打了去。那個老虎用嘴接住。嚼得粉碎。吞在肚子裏。照舊奔了他去。那個和尚更害怕了。連忙拿起經本子又對着老虎打了去咯。誰知那個老虎。看見是經本子趕緊的跑囘洞去。小虎兒看見了說。您去搜山。爲甚麼囘來的這麼快。老虎說今兒我好晦氣。偏偏兒的遇見了一個和尚。我繞吃了他兩片兒薄脆。他就把緣薄拿出來了。幸而我跑得快。要是一步兒來遲。我可拿甚麼佈施他呢。

第五十五陝西詩

有三個陝西人。在花園子裏閒坐。這個人說。偺們今兒閒着。為甚麼不每人作一首詩。那不有趣兒嗎。偺們就拿着園子裏的石榴竹子鷺鷥作個題目好不好。等我先作一首石榴詩。你們聽一聽。他就說了。青枝綠葉開紅花。咱家園裏也有他。三日兩日不看見。枝上結個大疙疸。那個人說。我作竹子詩。他說青枝綠葉不開花。咱家園裏也有他。有朝一日大風颳。革落革落又革落。這第三的說。石榴竹子都教你們作了。看看我的鷺鷥詩好不好。他說鷺鷥是。慣在水邊捉魚蝦。雪裏飛來不見他。他家老子咱認得頭上有個大紅疤。

第五十六 磕睡法

有一個奶媽子奶孩子。這個孩子愛哭。總不肯睡。奶媽子忽然想起一個主意來了。他就叫老爺老爺。拿本書來給

（念嘎拉）
（紅念渾）

第五十七 鋸酒盃

有一個客人。朋友家請他飲酒吃飯。偏是這位主人吝刻。每回斟酒不斟滿了。就斟半盃。客人可就和主人說。府上有鋸。拿一把來借我用用。主人說。正在吃喝的時候兒。您要鋸何用。客人就指着這個酒盃說。這個盃上半截兒既是盛不得酒咯。我替您鋸了去罷。留他空着半截兒作

我老爺說。你要書作甚麼呀。這個奶媽子說。我常常瞧見老爺不拿書便罷。要是拿起書來一看立刻可就睡着了。

第五十八 拳頭好得很

有一個外鄉人。在北京住了幾年。後來回了家咯。他無論提起甚麼來。總是誇北京的好。這天晚上同他父親在一塊兒走。旁邊兒有個人。可就說今兒晚上好月亮啊。這個誇嘴的聽見就說了。這兒的月亮。有甚麼好處。你們不知道京裏的那個月亮。纔好得很哪。他父親聽見很有氣。就罵着他說。天下共總就是一個月亮。怎麼獨北京的那麼甚麼呢。

好。說着話就照他兒子身上。給了一拳頭。他兒子挨了打。連哭帶喊的和他父親說。希罕你這個拳頭。你不知道北京城裏的那個拳頭。打上纔更好的狠哪。

第五十九蠢才

有哥兒倆。一同往朋友家去望看兄弟極糊塗。趕到了朋友家裏。入了坐了。底下人送上茶來。茶裏是用香桃作茶果兒。兄弟不認得。就悄悄兒的問他哥哥。這是甚麼東西。他哥哥說。蠢才。是因爲他糊塗。怕朋友見笑的意思。到了第二盅。人家又用橄欖泡茶。他又問他哥哥。這又是甚麼。他哥哥又說。蠡才。趕到後來出門回來了。兄弟就和他哥哥說。繞剛頭一個蠡才。雖然酸點兒。還有點兒甜味兒。到了第二個蠡才。是齁澀的。連一點兒甜味兒都沒咯。

第六十 門上貼道人

有一個人。因為新年去買門神爺。錯把個老道的畫兒買了來咯。就貼在門上了。他媳婦兒看見說。門神爺都是拿刀拿斧。畫的很凶惡。那鬼看見他繞怕哪。你把這個慈善的模樣兒貼在門上。有甚麼用處啊。他男人說。你別提咯。如今人的面貌兒。你瞧着他外面兒慈善。他行出來的事。是又毒又狠。

第六十一 面貌一樣

有一個人。抱着他的兒子。在街門口兒站着。傍邊有個好玩笑的。就指着這個孩子說。可見父子的骨血眞是一脈。就瞧你這個兒子的模樣兒長的怎麼就和我是一樣。一般無二。抱兒子的。就囘答他說。不錯。你和這個孩子。原是一個媽媽生出來的弟兄。這個面貌兒。長的怎麼不是一樣兒呢。

第六十二 粗月

有一個人常常兒的和人比論。無論是甚麼。總是用這個粗字兒自謙。這天請客。在家裏喝酒。喝到晚上了不覺的月亮就上來了。客人看見很喜歡。說今兒在您這兒想不到晚上有這麼樣兒的好月。這個人聽見。連忙的拱着手兒說。不敢當。不敢當。這不過是舍下的一個粗月兒。

第六十三 吃人不吐骨頭

有一個貓兒。閉着眼睛。嘴裏呼嚕呼嚕的。在那兒坐着有兩個耗子遠遠兒的看見。就悄不聲兒的說。貓爺爺今兒改惡向善了。在那兒念經哪。偺們可以出洞去遊玩遊玩。剛一出洞那貓趕上就拿住一個。連骨頭都吃了。那一個耗子趕緊的跑進洞去。告訴大夥兒說。我當是貓爺爺閉着眼兒念經。一定是變了善心了。那兒知道。行出來的事更狠。竟是個吃人不吐骨頭的。

第六十四 連我纔得三人

有一個念書的人狂傲無比。這天他對着別人說。聖人是最難出世的。當初盤古王。開天闢地。生人生萬物。誰能殼比他。屈起一個指頭來說。我要讓他為第一。末後兒到了孔夫子。刪詩書。定禮樂。出類拔萃。為萬代的師表。那個人不敬服他。可就又屈了一個指頭說。我只好讓他為第二咯。屈着兩個指頭說。除了這兩個人之後。再沒有可以屈得我的指頭的人了。說完了這個話想了半天。自己各兒。

點着頭兒說是啊。你說聖人難不難。可就叉屈一個指頭兒說。連我算上繞得三個人。

第六十五 少米少床

有一個窮人。對着衆人自誇說。我家雖不算得大富。然而舍下器物件件的不少。屈着一個指頭兒。所少者就是龍車鳳輦。要說吃的喝的樣樣兒俱全。叉屈了一個指頭說。所少者就是龍心鳳肝。他的小童兒。在傍邊搭了話了說。夜裏那兒來的床啊。就在地下鋪草睡覺。今兒晚上。連一個米粒兒都沒有。還在人前說大話哪。這個窮人聽說這話。抬起頭來想了一想說。是啊。是啊。我也忘了。我家裏到底兒是件件都有。所少者不過是龍心鳳肝晚飯米。龍車鳳輦夜裏的床。

第六十六 燒螞蟻用鄰箕

有一個好心的老太太兒。整天家手裏。掐着個誦珠兒。嘴裏頭高聲兒念的是阿彌陀佛。阿彌陀佛。這一天剛念完了佛。可就叫着他們家裏的孩子二漢說。你瞧這熱鍋上的螞蟻有多少。實在討人嫌。你拿火來。都把他給我燒死。說完了又高聲念了兩聲佛。剛念完這兩句。又叫二漢。你把鍋底下這個火灰。拿簸箕都把他撮出去。可千萬別使俙們家的。不看燒壞了。你拿俙們街坊張三的簸箕就行咯。

第六十七 要靴

陰司裏的判官靴子破了。到了陽間找了個皮匠。對他說。我給你二錢銀子定錢。你給我作雙新的。等作得了。我再找給你銀子，過了幾天，判官來取靴子來了。皮匠說，您前幾天給我的定銀，我纔買了幫兒，還沒有底兒哪，您遲幾天再來取罷。過了幾天又取靴子來咯。皮匠說，還沒有配得了底兒哪。判官連要了好幾囘，皮匠總說是沒底兒。這天閻王爺差小鬼把皮匠勾到陰司去了。閻王說，你這個皮匠，平日專會騙人的銀子，不肯就把東西交給人家，可惡極了，該下在油鍋地獄。只見要靴子那個判官，站在旁邊兒。皮匠就苦苦的哀求說，求您想個法子救我一救纔好。判官說不要緊。那個油鍋沒有底兒。扔下你去。你就可以逃跑了。夜叉過來拿起皮匠望油鍋裏一扔。那個皮匠連忙用手望四下里一摸。可就大嚷着說判官老爺。有底兒有底兒。那判官答了言說。你既說有底兒。為甚麼不把我的靴子給作得了。

第六十八 不打官司

有一個安徽人。連年的打官司。實在是怨恨。到了年底三十兒這天。父子爺兒三。計較計較。說明兒個初一就是新年。每人要說句吉祥的話兒。保佑着來年行好運不惹官司好不好。大兒子說。就請父親先說。他父親就說了今年好。大兒子跟着也說了。晦氣少。二兒子也說了。不得打官司。共是三句。十一個字。就寫了個紙條兒貼在堂屋裏。爲得是教人念誦。取個吉利兒。可巧清早女婿來拜年。瞧見了這個條兒就分作兩句。上五下六這麼一念說。今年好晦氣。少不得打官司。

第六十九 割股

有一個人。他父親病得利害。請了個大夫來瞧病。大夫說我看令尊的病。已然是無法可救。開個方兒試試看。除非你有孝心。割股煎藥。或者感動了天地。也可以緩得過來。他兒子說這個不難。趕到大夫走後。他就抽刀往外去了。這個時候兒又是個夏天。他就碰見一個人。在本人兒的屋門口兒。光着身子正睡覺呢。他就過去硬割了股肉一塊。這個人猛然驚醒就嚷起疼來咯。他擺着手兒說。你別嚷別嚷。你難道不知道割股救父是天地間最好的事麼。

第七十 看上你了

有一個糊塗大夫。成家之後。生了一個姑娘。一個小子。這天把人家兒子給治死了。人家不依。他就把他的兒子賠還人家了。可巧他又治死了別人的一個女孩兒。他就又把自己的姑娘。也賠了人家了。家裏頭就剩了他一個媳婦了。兩口子淒淒涼涼。正在那難過的時候兒。忽然又有人拍門請大夫。他就本人兒出去問那個人說給誰瞧病啊。那個人說。就是賤內。大夫進了屋子。哭着和他媳婦兒說。可不好了。准是有人又看上你了。

第七十一　看寫緣簿

有一個官兵。穿着布衣布靴。到一座廟裏去閒逛。和尚見他這個打扮兒。一定是個平常人。並沒有施禮款待。那個官兵。就和和尚說。我看你這個廟裏也狠淡薄。要是短甚麼裝修。拿緣簿來我好寫上佈施。和尚聽這個話。大喜立刻就獻茶。分外的恭敬起來了。連忙遞過緣簿打開。頭一行繞寫了總督部院四個字。和尚就當作他是個大官出來私行。不由的吃驚害怕。趕緊的就跪下了。這個人又在總督部院四個字底下。又添寫標下左營官兵。和尚一見是個官兵啊。就惱了。趕緊的站起來。就立而不跪了。又見他在緣簿上。添寫你施三十四個字。和尚心想着必是三十兩銀子。又一喜歡。從新又跪下了。這個人又在三十底下。添寫文錢兩個字。和尚見他你施的太少。隨又站起來把身子一扭。立刻就喜變成怒。背地裏生氣去了。

第七十二兄弟合種田

有這麼哥兒倆。夥種田地。到了秋收的時候兒。兄弟要和哥哥分稻子。哥哥可就和兄弟說。咱們是骨肉弟兄。何必這麼樣兒的瑣碎。教傍人瞧着咱們這麼彼此的較量實在是不好看。莫若今年我收上頭的稻米。你收底下的稻草。趕到明年我得下頭的。你得上頭的。咱們倆一遞一年的。何等的公道。兄弟說。就是這麼樣罷。到了第二年春天了。兄弟可就和哥哥說。眼下該栽秧兒了。哥哥說。你別忙。我聽見人說。今年必要大旱。咱們改種芋頭罷。可是記着去年我說過的那個話。今年我收下頭的了。這纏教作公道良心。一遞一年的。永遠不許改換就是了。

第七十三 茶飯不週全

有一個嫖客。把銀錢全都花淨敗了家了。他就挨着門兒唱曲兒要飯。糊口過日子。這一天從他早認識的一個妓女門口兒過。聽見這個姑娘陪着客人在裏頭喝酒。又低着聲兒唱。唱的是我為你清滅了桃花面。這一句。他就在門口兒。猛然的高聲接着唱說。我為你茶飯不週全。

第七十四 方蛇

有一個人這天頭一囘瞧見一條大長蟲。他就說大話告訴別人說。這條長蟲寬裏下有十丈長裏下毀一百丈。這個人說。我斷不信。說大話的人又說了。不到一百丈。也有五十丈了。那個人說。我還是不信。他又減着說有三十丈罷。二十丈罷。末末了兒減到十丈了。他自各兒恍然大悟。說我錯了我錯了。要照着我這麼說。噯呀。這不成了一個長方兒的長蟲了麼。

第七十五 鹹蛋

有一個鄉下人。來在城裏頭。這天有個朋友請他吃飯菜裏頭有一碟兒鹹鴨蛋。他吃在嘴裏頭說。奇怪呀。怎麼這個蛋他會鹹了呢。他的朋友就告訴他說。你不知道我們北京城裏專有一種鹹鴨子。所以下出來的蛋。他自然也是鹹的了。

第七十六 扣除二兩一夜

有一個老頭兒。慈善好施捨。這天下大雪。見一個窮人在他街門口兒房簷兒底下站着避雪。老頭兒見他凍的可憐。就把他讓進屋子裏頭了。給他燙酒趕寒。留他住了一夜。到了第二天。那個雪還是不住。又把他留下了。一連三天。這天天也晴了。這個人臨要走的時候兒。可就和老頭兒說。把您的刀借給我使使。老頭兒把刀遞給他。他接刀在手。對着老頭兒說。俗們倆素不相識。承您哪這個樣兒的美意。惟有殺身報恩就結了。老頭兒聽他這個話。嚇了一跳。連忙攔住說。要像這麼樣你不是報恩。反是害了我了。這個人說。怎麼是害您哪老頭兒說。我家裏就這麼死了個人。要是一點事兒沒有。少說着燒埋銀也得花十二兩。零碎使費那還在外。這個人說承您的厚情。不用算那些個使費。您就把燒埋銀十二兩給我我走了老頭兒聽這話狠有氣。就嚷起來了。驚動了街坊四鄰出來給他們說合。竟作情一半。給了他六兩。這個人剛拿着要走老頭兒看見就嘆口氣說誰想到遇見這麼樣兒的沒良心的人。這個人說。不說你自己沒良心。反倒說我沒良心。老頭兒說。怎麼是我沒良心。這個人說。你旣是有良心就不該當那麼折算。我共總住了三夜。就扣除我二兩銀子一夜。那還算有良心嗎。

第七十七女勾死鬼

閻王爺差了一名勾死鬼兒。到陽世間去勾人。這個勾死鬼兒。獨自一個空身兒回來咯。閻王爺就問他。你不把某人給我勾了來。是甚麼緣故。那勾死鬼兒說。回老爺的話。這個人身邊現在有兩個狠標緻的娘兒們。天天兒跟着他呢。比我這勾死鬼兒更利害。小的想不幾天兒的功夫。他自己就來咯。又何必勾他去呢。

第七十八囬債

有一個人該人家的銀子有許多日子不還這天可巧在半道兒上。遇見借銀子的主兒了。要定了說。你借我的銀子有多少天。今兒可該還我了。欠主兒說遲是遲了。我這兒有個比方。你要是明白了。自然就不和我要了。譬如我這個銀子前日已經還了你了。自然你拿去也就花完了。

難道說你還和我要麼。銀子主兒說。你這教蠻話。你要是還了我。我又在別處生利錢去了。欠債的人說。你說我這個話不通。還有一說。譬如我出了外咯。你也來找我要銀子麼。銀子主兒說。少不得等你囘來我更要的利害。欠主兒又說。我勸你只當我遠處去咯。沒有囘來。自然你得多等幾天兒再要。銀子主兒說。你現時在我眼頭裏哪。怎麼說沒有囘來。欠主兒說。還有一說。你再再的一定教我還銀子。我沒有銀子還你。自然就得打架。設若一拳你把我打死了。那個時候兒。你得不着銀子。反要經官受刑。一定破家蕩產。坐監償命。你那就後悔不來了。就是我打死你罷。我也得受罪抵償。難道說你還能殻死而復生。再和我要銀子麼。今兒你我一見任話不提。安安靜靜兒的那不舒服麼。何苦定要打罵自尋苦惱呢。銀子主兒的那不極了說憑你怎麼會說。我就要你還銀子。欠主兒也大嚷着說。我說了多少好話你都不聽。無論你怎麼會要。我就是不還你銀子。

第七十九 偷酒

有一位教書的先生好喝酒。他的下人最愛偷酒。偷的先生直不敢用人咯。這天先生自己各兒打算。說總得找一個不會喝酒的。縱不能偷。然而還得找一個不認得酒的。那縱是眞不偷。這天朋友薦了個人來。先生就拿着黃酒問他。那個人說這是陳紹。先生說酒的名兒出處。他都知道。如何能不會喝呢。立刻就把他打發了。隨後又薦了一個來。先生還是拿着黃酒問他。他說這准是花雕罷。先生說連酒的美品。他都叫的上來。斷不是個不會喝的。可就立刻把他辭了。到後來又薦一個人來。一進門兒就拿着黃酒問他。他說不認得。又拿起燒酒來問他。他又說不知道這叫甚麼。先生聽了很喜歡。以爲這個人是一定不會喝酒的個人咯。可就把他留下了。這天先生要出門。留他看家。就囑咐他說牆上掛的火腿。院裏的肥雞。你要小心看着屋子裏有倆瓶。一瓶是白砒。一瓶是紅砒。萬萬不可動他。要是喝了肝腸寸斷。一定准死。叮嚀了再三。這纔走了。先生走後。他就殺雞煮腿。把兩瓶酒。挨次兒喝完。不覺大醉。他就躺在地下咯。趕到先生回來。推門兒一瞧。見底下人倒臥在地。又見火腿肥雞也全沒了。不由得怒氣攻心。把底下人踢醒了。細細兒的究問他。他繞哭着說了。主人走後小人原是用心看守。想不到來了一個貓。把火腿叨了去咯。忽然又跑進一條狗來。把肥雞追的也沒了影兒咯。小人是眞氣極了不願意活着了。可就想起您臨走吩咐的話來了。說紅白二砒。喝要了命。小的先把紅砒喝乾了。心裏不覺怎麼樣。後來把白砒也都喝淨了。還是不能死。現在小的是頭暈腦悶。弄的不死不活躺在這兒掙命哪。

第八十 千金子

有一個人。手裏有一千兩金子。這天遇着個窮人。和他誇富。狂傲着說。我富有千金。你爲甚麼不奉承我。那個窮人說。你有千金是你的。與我甚麼相干。我奉承你作甚麼。這個有金子的人說。我分給你一半兒。你該奉承我了罷。窮人更會說。你既有一千兩金子。你留五百。分我五百。倆們倆平等。是一個樣的數兒。我又何必奉承你呢。有金子的說。我可着整數兒把這一千都送給你。難到說還不該奉承我嗎。窮人說你的千金我得了來咯。你應當奉承我纔是。我更不必奉承你了。

第八十一 當屬問答

有一個捐班出身的知縣。不懂得官話。到任後謁見上司。上司就問他。貴縣風土何如。他回答說並無大風更少塵又問他春花何如。他說今春的棉花。每勉二百八十。上司又問他紳糧何如。他回答說卑職的身量足穿三尺六。又問他那兒的百姓怎麼樣。他說白杏就有兩棵紅杏却到不少。上司說我問的是黎庶。他說黎樹多極了。結果子的很少。上司說我不是問甚麼黎杏。我是問你的小民知縣他連忙跕起來說。卑職的小名兒叫狗兒。

第八十二問靴價

有一個慢性兒的人買了雙新靴子。就遇見個急性子人問他。說老兄這靴子是多少銀子買的。那個慢性兒的人。就慢條斯理兒的。伸出一隻腳來。告訴他說二兩四錢。這個急性子人一聽。揪住他的家人就打。說好大膽的奴才。你給我買的這雙靴子。因為甚麼要四兩八錢。像你這個樣兒的賺錢欺主。實在是可惡極了。慢性兒的在傍解勸。說老兄有話慢慢兒說。何必動這麼大氣說完了這個話。他又慢慢兒的。伸出一隻腳來。說老兄這一隻也是二兩四錢。

第八十三 爵譚

爵位分作五等。是公侯伯子男。要是功勞在五等以上的人。就可以封王。想當初優待有功之臣是何等樣兒的尊貴。到如今年代兒也遠了。勢派兒也就低微的狠咯。那個窮不敢品的。較比那閑散的人更利害。就有人用那音同字不同的這個話耍戲着說他們。甚麼叫公。了頭老婆硬上弓。甚麼叫侯。一毛兒不拔白吃猴。甚麼叫伯。胡吹混嗙慣說白。甚麼叫子。寡廉鮮恥無賴子。甚麼叫男。少吃無穿實在難。甚麽叫王。窮凶極惡等閒亡。

第八十四問猴

有一位縣太爺謁見上司。談完了公事。和上司閒說話兒上司就問他。說貴縣那個地方兒出猴子不知都有多大。他回答說頂大的有大人那麽大。敢到說出來了自知失言。心裏覺着害怕趕緊的站起來說就是至小的。也有卑職那麽大。

第八十五十萬富

有一個人。他有十萬之富。這天他和一個貧人自誇。說我富有十萬。你知道不知道。那個貧人說。我也有十萬。這算不了甚麼希罕事啊。富人說。你的十萬在甚麼地方哪。那個貧人說了。你素日有了不肯用。我要用沒得用。那還不是一樣嗎。

第八十六 大嘡小嘡

北京城裏好說大話薰人的。那就叫作嘡。東城有個大嘡。西城有個小嘡。這天小嘡找了大嘡去。要爲難爲難他。說你的外號兒叫大唥。你能唥動了老虎。我就拜你爲師。大唥說這有何難。你要不信偺們立刻找老虎去。說着話倆人一同進了深山。來找虎窩。小唥說這個地方兒。就是虎豹來往之處。你在這兒等老虎。我上山去看你怎麼個唥法兒。大唥就靠着樹一坐。忽然見一隻老虎咆哮而來。大唥忙同手。拔了一棵小柳樹拿着就唥開了。說我剛纔吃了一隻豹。又找補了一隻虎。誰知虎老肉柴。塞了我的牙咯。一邊兒說着。一邊兒就拿柳樹。做出個剔牙的樣子來。

老虎一聽回頭就跑。逃回洞去。遇見了一個猴兒。老虎就和他說。好利害人。吃了一豹一虎。在那兒拿柳樹剔牙哪。我如何敢吃他。還怕他要吃我哪。猴兒說你也太膽兒小了。我要和你去看一看到底是怎麼樣兒的一個人。老虎說我不放心。你要同去。總得把你拴在我的脊梁上猴兒也答應了。老虎把猴兒拴好。騎在老虎的身上。來到大嗙的跟前兒。大嗙看見就高聲大罵。說好個撒謊的猴兒崽子。昨兒我拿住你要吃。你是苦苦的哀求我。許下今兒一早。給我送兩隻老虎。兩個豹來供我的早飯。萬想不到天這早晚兒。就送這麼一隻瘦山貓來搪塞我。老虎一聽這個話。說了不得了。我受了猴兒的誆騙了。囘頭就跑。誰知老虎跑得快。猴兒騎不住掉下虎去。又教樹根子。把猴兒掛住弄兩截咯。老虎身上就剩下一個猴兒腦袋了。老虎跑囘洞去。喘了半天。囘頭來找猴子。就見繩子上拴着個猴兒頭。老虎吃這一驚不小。說幸虧我跑得快。饒這麼樣。還把猴兒的下半截兒。給留下了。

第八十七 蘇空頭

有一個北京人。頭一囘上蘇州去。別人就告訴他說。那兒的本地人慣會鬧空頭。你要去買貨。他要是要二兩。你就還他一兩。就是和人說話。他說兩句。也只好聽他一句。這個京裏人。到了蘇州咯。先拿買貨子法子試一試。果然給了一半兒的價錢就賣了。後來遇見個本地人。就問他貴姓。他說姓陸。京裏人說。想來定是老三了。又問他住宅房子幾間。他說五間。京裏人說。原來是兩間半了。又問宅上還有甚麼人。他說就有一個媳婦兒。京裏人又說。想來是倆人夥娶的罷。

第八十八 恍忽

有一個人錯穿了靴子。一隻底兒厚。一隻底子薄。走起道兒來。是一腳高一腳低。狠不合式。這個人就自各兒詫異。說今兒我的腿。爲甚麼一長一短。想是道兒不平的原故罷。別人就告訴他說。閣下准是錯穿了靴子咯。他就忙叫家人囘家取去。家人去了半天。還是空着手兒囘來了。告訴老爺說。不用換了家裏的那兩隻。也是一薄一厚。

第八十九 寫別字

有一個人愛寫白字。寫字的時候兒。還是愛錯。這天因為他大舅子害眼。打算要寫個信去問候問候。又恐怕寫了錯字。可就問朋友說舅字怎麼寫。朋友說一直一個日字。他就把一直。挪在日字底下了。寫成一個旦字。又問茄字怎麼寫。朋友說草字頭兒底下一個加字。他又錯寫了家人的家字。寫成一個蒙字。後來又問眼字怎麼寫。朋友說目字傍兒加上一個艮字。他又錯寫樹木的那個木字。都寫得了一看。寫的是信寄大旦子。千萬別吃秋後蒙。要是吃了秋後蒙。恐怕害了大旦子的根。

第九十 大蚊

有一個人出外去了。回到家來。就對着他媳婦兒說。我到燕子磯。蚊蟲大如雞。後過巫山峽。蚊子大如鴨。他媳婦兒說我不信。會有這麼大蚊子。他男人說。那一夜我在帳子裏睡覺。來了個蚊子。他把腦袋鑽進帳子裏頭。教我一把就搹住他的脖子了。老沒有放。急的那個蚊子在帳子外頭。倆翅膀兒直搧了一夜。倒很凉快。他媳婦說。你旣搹住。爲甚麼不把他帶回來給我吃呢。他男人說。求着他不吃我。就殼了。你還想要吃他。

第九十一 弟兄兩謊

有把弟把兄。兩個人都愛說謊話。這一天把兄告訴把弟說。我昨兒吃了個極大的煮餑餑。再也沒他大的咯。一百勋麵。八十勋肉。二十勋菜。包了一個。煮得了。用八張方棹。

纔擱的下他。二十幾個人。四面兒轉着吃。吃了一天一夜。還沒吃到一半兒哪。正吃的高興。不見了倆人。各處尋找。踪影全無。忽然聽見煮餑餑皮兒裏有人說話。揭開皮兒一瞧。那倆人鑽在裏頭。掏餡兒吃呢。你說大不大。把弟說。我昨兒也吃了個頂大的肉包子。那纔算得是大呢。幾十人吃了三天三夜。還沒瞧見餡兒哪。就望裏緊着這麼一吃。吃出一塊石碑來。碑上寫着離餡子還有三十里。你看這個包子大不大。把兒就問他。說你這個大包子。拿甚麼鍋蒸的。把弟說。就是用您下煮餑餑的那口鍋。

第九十二 談天

有眾客人。湊到一塊兒談天兒。論天的度數。遠近有多少。各人有各自的說法兒。大家分辯。總不能決斷。傍邊兒有個樵夫說我可以分解。要說天離着地的遠近。也就在三四百里。打下往上去。慢慢兒走四天可到。要是快走三天就到了。六七天的工夫。打個來囘。綽綽有餘。眾位為甚麼這麼分爭不能決斷呢。眾客人聽他這個話就一愣。可就問他。要依你這麼說。甚麼是個對證。樵夫說。諸位難道不知世間上到了臘月二十三。家家兒祭竈送竈王爺上天這個風俗麼。二十三送上天去。到了三十兒又接竈王囘來。打二十三到三十兒。不過七天。用一半兒的道兒算計。繞三四百里地。有甚麼遠的呢。衆客人一聽。他這個算法兒。不由的鬨堂大笑。說你說的很是。足可以談天。

第九十三死錯了人

有一個人。他的親家母死了。託教學的先生作篇祭文。這位先生。就找出舊文集事這本書來。抄了一篇祭親家公的祭文給他。這個人接過來一瞧說錯了。先生聽他說錯了。就狠有氣。說我告訴你。這篇祭文。是刻在書上的。一個字也不能錯。除非是他們家。死錯了人咯。

第九十四 打個半死

有一個極寒苦的人。這天遇見個財主。就和他說。我送給你一千兩銀子。我可得把你活活兒的打死。這個窮人。想了牛天。說您就給我五百兩。打我個半死兒罷。

第九十五 醫駝背

有一個大夫自誇。專能治羅鍋子。就是腰灣的像張弓。彷彿蝦米似的。請我一治。立刻就能筆管兒調直。可巧有個羅鍋子信他的話。請他給治。他就搬出兩片大木板來。拿一片放在地下。叫羅鍋子仰八腳兒躺在板上。又拿一塊板。給羅鍋子壓在身上。兩頭兒用粗繩子緊勒緊收。那羅鍋子疼極了。就大嚷着說。我不治了鬆開我罷。大夫不聽他的話。反到上板子上站着。加着勁兒。重重的用脚蹬。

他。這個羅鍋子的腰雖然直了。可是沒了氣兒咯。傍邊兒的人揪住大夫不依。說你爲甚麼把他治死了。大夫說。我就知道給他把腰治直了。我那兒管他的死活呢。

第九十六 溺水

有一個人。掉在水裏了。他兒子大聲嚷着說。快來救人哪。救上來。我必重重兒的謝候他。他父親在水裏。也探出頭來。高聲的喊叫。說要是三分銀子。便來救我。若是要的多。教他們不必來救。

第九十七 剩個窮花子與我

有姓張姓李的。兩個人這天在一塊兒走。遇見一個坐轎的富翁帶着多少的跟人。姓張的就把姓李的拉住。往人家門後頭躲避。告訴他說。這轎子裏坐的。是我的至親。若不躲他。他就得下轎給我行禮。彼此的勞動。豈不費事。姓李的說。那是應該躲避的。倆人說着話。又往前走。不大的工夫兒。又遇見一個騎馬的貴人。衣帽鮮明。跟的人也不少。姓張的又把姓李的拉着躲在人家門後頭。說這個騎馬的。是我自幼兒的好朋友。我要是不躲他。他總得下來。給我請安。彼此還是費事。姓李的說。這也是應該躲着的。說着話仍往前走。從老遠的看見一個花子。破衣破帽。喊叫着來咯。姓李的說快走。拉住姓張的。也往人家門後頭躲避。說你瞧這個花子。不但是我的至親。而且還是好友。我要是不避諱他。他看見我。豈不臉上討愧麼。姓張的聽說很詫異。說你怎麼有這個樣兒的至親好友哪。姓李的說。富的貴的。都教你佔了去咯。就剩個窮花子給我了。我

第九十八 大澡盆

有兩個外路客人。遇在一塊兒咯。各人說本地的奇怪事。這個客人說。做處有個洗澡盆。可容千數多人。在裏頭洗澡。那個客人說。這個盆還不算奇。做處有根竹竿子。長得上拄天下拄地。長到天上沒有地方咯。又灣回來。還是朝着地。那纔算得是奇事呢。先前那個客人就問咯。那兒有那麼大竹竿子。這個客人說。若沒我這根大竹子。怎麼能和他混混罷。

篦你那個大澡盆呢。

第九十九 剪箭桿

有一個當兵的。中了箭了。疼痛難忍。就請了位出名的外科給他治。這位一瞧。說不難不難很容易治。他就拿了把大剪子。把外頭露着的箭桿子。齊齊兒的。給他鉸了去咯。他就要馬錢要走。那個兵說。箭桿兒雖然鉸了去了。箭頭兒還在肉裏頭哪。怎麼不給我治出來。就要走呢。這個外科搖着頭說我不管。我們外科的治法。算完了事了。這個箭頭兒在肉裏頭哪。那是內科的事。怎麼也教我們外科給治呢。

CHINESE FOLKLORE

PEKINESE RHYMES

FIRST COLLECTED AND EDITED WITH

NOTES AND TRANSLATION

BY

BARON GUIDO VITALE

CHINESE SECRETARY TO THE ITALIAN LEGATION.

PEKING.

PEI-T'ANG PRESS

1896.

TO

PROFESSOR LODOVICO NOCENTINI

IN

SIGN OF ESTEEM AND FRIENDSHIP

PREFACE

I bring for the first time to light a collection of Pekinese children-rhymes with the conviction that the reader may gather from the lecture these benefits.

1º. The acquirement of a small treasure of words and phrases hardly to be met with elsewhere.

2º. A clearer insight into scenes and details of chinese common life.

3º. The notion that some true poetry may be found in chinese popular songs.

These rhymes have no known authors; some of them are perhaps composed by mothers watching at children's bedside, others may be composed by naughty school-boys when the teacher is having his nap over a page of the great philosopher. At all events they are like wild flowers which spring up nobody knows how and when and fade and die in the same way.

The trouble in collecting them was far greater than I had thought. "Tabood" as we are in Peking, where could I go myself to hear the rhymes and note them down?

Then I had recourse to my teacher, but as he thinks to be a literary man, he grew quite indignant at my proposal, and assured and pledged that no such rubbish had ever existed in China. However as I happened (of course by chance) to take out of my drawer some dollars, and place them beneath his reach, he suddenly abated his furors and mumbled that "perhaps I was not mistaken and that of course he would by every possible mean try to get what I wanted".

And I shall say to his justice that he kept his word and the dollars. But when he had collected forty or so, his stock was quite exhausted and I had to look for other helps.

In summer time residing in temples in the neighbourhood of Peking I had large chance of intercourse with the people and could increase my stock of rhymes. I was furthermore able to improve the former texts and to reprove all those which being not matched by oral testimony were probably spurious.

After the work of collection, came the work of explanation and translation which was not always easy. The people who spoke the words often were not able to give me light on the difficult points. When pressed by me they suggested something and I picked up what looked more truthlike and reasonable; never did I force or prefer views of my own.

Somebody will object to my statement that sparkles of true poetry are to be found in this book. That will very naturally happen to all those who are entirely foreign to the chinese world. Several rhymes (however few in proportion to the bulk of the book)[1] are simple and touching and may be "poetry" for those who have even a slight knowledge of chinese joys and sorrows.

I shall draw also the reader's attention to the system of versification followed in these rhymes. Composed as they are by illiterate people who have no notion of written language, they show a system of versification analogous to that of many European countries, and almost completely agreeing with the rules

---

[1] 3.9.10.11.13.15.23.32.43.44.53.54.55.60.91.117.123.125.

of the Italian poetry. A new national poetry could perhaps spring up based on these rhythms and on the true feelings of the people.

I took every pain to collect the most I could, yet the work could be by far richer than it is. Those who live in freeer intercourse with the people could easily add numerous and fine samples of this uncultivated poetry. I would be extremely pleased if any one would either furnish to me new materials, or would himself undertake the work of a new collection of rhymes.

Any critic, advise or literary contribution will be gratefully received by the author.

I am glad to be able to express here my deep feelings of gratitude to Mr. A. M. C. Raab of the British Legation, who kindly undertook the revision of almost the whole manuscript and to Mr. Krebs of the German Legation who kindly helped me in correcting the proofs.

BARON GUIDO VITALE
Italian Legation.

Peking. 30th September 1896.

INDEX.

Chang¹ ta⁴ sao³	Pag. 23	張大嫂
Che⁴ ko⁴ jen² sheng¹ lai²	192	這個人生來性兒急
Cheng¹ yüe⁴ li³ cheng¹ yüe⁴ cheng¹	195	正月裏正月正
Chi⁴ tsao⁴ chi⁴ tsao⁴	170	祭竈祭竈新年來到
Chiao¹ ni² pan⁴ 'r	169	膠泥瓣兒
Chie¹ cho ch'iang² 'eur	165	隔着牆兒扔切糕
Chih⁴ chi¹ ling²	100	雉鷄翎
Chin¹ ku¹ lu¹ pang⁴	34	金軲轆棒
Ch'in² shih³ huang²	184	秦始皇
Ching¹ t'iao² kun⁴ 'r	88	荊條棍兒
Ch'iung² t'ai⁴ t'ai⁴ 'r	193	窮太太兒
Ch'o³ ch'o³	35	扯扯
Ch'u¹ la men²	52	出了門兒
Ch'u¹ la men² 'r hao³ sang⁴ ch'i⁴	145	出了門兒好喪氣
Ch'u¹ i¹ ch'u¹ eur⁴ ch'u¹ san¹ ssu⁴	207	初一初二初三四兒
Ch'ü³ hsi² fu⁴ 'r ti	90	娶媳婦兒的
Chui¹ pang¹ tzu³ 'r	189	錐幫子兒
Fan¹ ping³ lao⁴ ping³	78	翻餅烙餅
Feng¹ lai² la	103	風來咯
Han² ya¹ 'r han² ya¹ 'r kuo⁴	21	寒鴉兒寒鴉兒過
Hao² jo⁴ t'ien¹ 'r	116	好熱天兒
Hao¹ tzu teng¹	133	蒿子燈
Hei¹ lao³ p'ouo² 'r	125	黑老婆兒
Ho² shang⁴ ho² shang⁴ iao² ling² tang⁴	67	和尙和尙搖鈴鐺

Hou⁴ ti³ 'r hsie²	80	厚底兒鞋
Hu¹ hu¹	95	糊糊
Hua¹ hung² liou³ lu⁴ hsien⁴ 'r	64	花紅柳綠線兒
Huai² shu⁴ huai²	31	槐樹槐
Huang² kou³ huang² kou³	17	黃狗黃狗你看家
Huang² ch'eng² ken¹ 'r	128	黃城根兒
Huang² tou⁴ li⁴ 'r	175	黃豆粒兒
Hung² to² li	201	紅得哩
Hung² hu² lu²	84	紅葫蘆
Hsi³ ch'iao³ i³ pa¹ ch'ang²	92	喜雀尾巴長
Hsi³ 'r hsi³ 'r ch'ih¹ tou⁴ fu³	138	喜兒喜兒吃豆腐
Hsi³ 'r hsi³ 'r mai³ tou⁴ fu³	139	喜兒喜兒買豆腐
Hsi¹ hsi¹ chiao¹	185	蹊蹊蹺
Hsi³ hua¹ ch'ia¹ lai² tai⁴ man³ t'ou²	188	喜花揩來戴滿頭
Hsi³ 'r hsi³ 'r	198	喜兒喜兒
Hsiang¹ hsiang¹ hao¹ tzu	46	香香蒿子
Hsiang¹ lu² 'r	105	香爐兒
Hsiao³ t'u¹ 'r	10	小禿兒
Hsiao³ pai² ts'ai⁴	22	小白菜兒
Hsiao³ eur⁴ ko¹	32	小二哥
Hsiao³ u³ 'r	42	小五兒
Hsiao³ hsiao³ tzu	44	小小子
Hsiao³ hui² hui² 'r	68	小回回兒
Hsiao³ t'u¹ 'r	93	小禿兒
Hsiao³ niu¹ 'r	106	小妞兒
Hsiao³ chiao³ 'r niang²	107	小脚兒娘
Hsiao³ hsiao³ tzu	113	小小子兒
Hsiao³ hsiao³ tzu	127	小小子兒

Hsiao³ ch'in² chiao¹	131	小秦椒兒
Hsiao³ san¹ 'r t'a¹ ma¹	134	小三兒他媽
Hsiao³ hao⁴ tzu	135	小耗子兒
Hsiao³ ta⁴ chie³	142	小大姐
Hsiao³ yüan² 'r	149	小元兒
Hsiao³ san¹ 'r, hsiao³ san¹ 'r	164	小三兒小三兒
Hsiao³ t'ao² ch'i⁴	179	小陶氣兒
Hsiao³ ta⁴ chie³	187	小大姐
Hsiao³ hsiao³ tzu k'ai¹ p'u⁴ 'r	196	小小子開鋪兒
Hsiao³ ku¹ niang² tsuo⁴ i¹ meng⁴	196	小姑娘作一夢
Hsiao³ p'ang⁴ hsiao³ tzu	204	小胖小子兒
Hsiao³ p'ang⁴ ko¹	219	小胖哥
Hsin¹ ta³ i¹ pa³ ch'a₂ hu²	65	新打一把茶壺
Hsin¹ ku¹ niang² shih² chi³ la	143	新姑娘十幾咯
I¹ chin⁴ men² hsi³ ch'ung¹ ch'ung¹	66	一進門兒喜冲冲
I¹ ya¹ eur⁴ ya¹	69	一呀二呀
I¹ fu⁴ k'uang¹	77	一副筐
I¹ chin⁴ men² 'r hei¹ ku¹ lung¹ tung²	147	一進門兒黑咕窿咚
I¹ ko⁴ chien¹ 'r	176	一個毽兒
Jih⁴ t'ou² ch'u¹ lai² i¹ tien³ hung²	25	日頭出來一點紅
Kao¹ kao¹ shan¹ shang⁴ you³ i¹ chia¹	45	高高山上有一家
Kao¹ kao¹ shan¹ shang⁴ i¹ tsuo⁴ hsiao³ miao⁴	64	高高山上一座小廟
Kao¹ kao¹ shan¹ shang⁴ i¹ luo⁴ chuan¹	79	高高山上一落磚
Kao¹ kao¹ shan¹ shang⁴ i¹ k'o¹ hao¹	104	高高山上一顆蒿
Kao¹ kao¹ shan¹ shang⁴ i¹ tsuo⁴ lou²	108	高高山上一座樓

Kao¹ kao¹ shan¹ shang⁴ i¹ k'o¹ ma²	116	高高山上一顆蔴
Kao¹ kao¹ shan¹ shang⁴ iou³ ko⁴ hsiao³ miao⁴	119	高高山上有個小廟
Kao¹ kao¹ shan¹ shang⁴ i¹ tsuo⁴ lou²	148	高高山上一座樓
Kao¹ kao¹ shan¹ shang⁴ i¹ uo¹ chu¹	190	高高山上一窩猪
Kao¹ kao¹ shan¹ shang⁴ i¹ ko⁴ niu²	205	高高山上一個牛
Ken¹ 'r ken¹ 'r	152	哏兒哏兒
Ku⁴ pu⁴ to² i¹ shih² shuei⁴ chao² la	139	顧不得一時睡着
Ku³ k'ao⁴ cho² ku³ lai²	199	鼓靠着鼓來
Ku¹ tung¹ tung¹	247	轂洞洞
La¹ ta⁴ chü⁴	1	拉大鋸
La¹ la¹ ku³ ti¹ ch'o¹ san¹ ko¹ ko¹	162	拉拉穀的車三哥哥
Lan² tien⁴ ch'ang³	101	藍靛廠
Lao³ t'ai⁴ t'ai⁴ chiao⁴ mao¹	130	老太太叫貓
Li⁴ la ch'iu¹ lai² li⁴ la ch'iu¹	40	立了秋來立了秋
Li⁴ li⁴ li⁴ li⁴ chan⁴ 'r	123	立立立立站兒
Liang³ chih¹ la⁴	135	兩枝蠟
Ling² lung² t'a³	98	玲瓏塔
Luo² kuo¹ tzu ch'iao²	55	羅鍋子橋
Luo⁴ t'o² luo⁴ t'o² so⁴ so⁴	110	駱駝駱駝嗉嗉
Luo² kuo¹ 'r ch'iao²	124	羅鍋兒橋
Ma² tzu³ ma²	12	痲子痲
Ma² tzu³ kuei³	137	痲子鬼
Mai³ i¹ pao¹	206	買一包
Mei² mu⁴ 'r	97	煤糢兒
Men² 'r ch'iao¹ ti pang¹ pang¹	178	門兒敲的梆梆
Miao⁴ li³ ti ho² shang⁴ la¹ ta⁴ suo³	166	廟裏的和尚拉大鎖
Miao⁴ men² tuei⁴ miao⁴ men² 'r	191	廟門對廟門兒

Mie¹ mie¹ yang²	62	咩咩羊
Muo⁴ li⁴ hua¹ 'r ti chang⁴ fu¹	153	茉莉花兒的丈夫
Nan² ching¹ ta⁴ liou³ shu⁴	216	南京大柳樹
Ni² ni² ni² ni² puo¹ puo¹	47	泥泥泥泥餑餑
Ni³ ma¹ ch'i¹	111	你媽七
Ni³ iao⁴ sha² ni³ iao⁴ sha²	208	你要奢你要奢
Niao¹ niao¹ niao¹	192	鳥鳥鳥
Nien² nien² iou³ ko⁴ san¹ yüe⁴ san¹	215	年年有個三月三
Niu¹ 'r iao⁴ ch'ih¹ mien⁴	49	妞兒要吃麪
Pa¹ hsien¹ chuo¹ 'r	137	八仙棹兒
Pai² t'a³ ssu⁴	186	白塔寺
Pien1¹ p'ao⁴ i¹ hsiang³ pa⁴ chang¹ k'ai²	209	鞭炮一响把張開
P'ing² tso² men² la¹ ta⁴ kung¹	155	平則門拉大弓
San¹ 'r san¹ 'r	60	三兒三兒
Sung¹ chih¹ 'r shu⁴	173	松枝兒樹
Sung¹ pai³ chih¹ 'r	176	松柏枝兒
Sha¹ t'u³ ti⁴ 'r	9	沙土地兒
Shang⁴ ku¹ lu⁴ t'ai²	2	上軲轆台
Shih² liou⁴ hua¹ 'r ti chie³	28	石榴花兒的姐
Shih⁴ shui² p'ai¹ uo³ ti men² 'r	194	是誰拍我的門兒
Shou⁴ hsing¹ lao³ 'r fu² lu⁴ hsing¹	219	壽星老兒福祿星
Shu⁴ ye⁴ 'r ch'ing¹	38	樹葉兒青
Shu⁴ ye⁴ 'r hei¹	78	樹葉兒黑
Shui² ken¹ uo³ uan² 'r	14	誰跟我頑兒
Shuei³ niu² 'r shuei³ niu² 'r	48	水牛兒水牛兒
Shuo¹ k'ai¹ ch'uan² chiou⁴ k'ai¹ ch'uan²	161	說開船就開船

Ta¹ lien² 'r ta¹	53	褡連兒搭
Ta¹ lien² 'r ta¹	59	褡連兒搭
Ta³ hua¹ pa¹ chang³	72	打花巴掌
Ta³ luo² 'r shai¹	76	打羅兒篩
Ta³ luo² 'r shai¹	180	打羅兒篩
Ta⁴ t'u¹ tzu³ to² ping⁴	36	大禿子得病
Ta⁴ niang² tzu³ ho¹ chiou³	57	大娘子喝酒
Ta⁴ fan¹ ch'o¹	63	大翻車
Ta⁴ ko¹ ko¹ eur⁴ ko¹ ko¹	194	大哥哥二哥哥
Ta⁴ niang² eur⁴ niang² ts'ai¹	202	大娘二娘猜
T'ao² shu⁴ ye⁴ 'r chien¹	112	桃樹葉兒尖
Ti¹ ti¹ ti¹	171	滴滴滴
T'i⁴ teng¹ kun¹ 'r	27	剔燈棍兒
T'iao¹ shuei³ ti ko¹	7	挑水的哥
T'ien¹ huang² huang²	241	天皇皇
T'ie³ ts'an² tou⁴	89	鐵蠶豆
Tou⁴ ya² ts'ai⁴	183	豆芽菜
T'ou² pien¹ hui¹	213	頭遍灰
T'u¹ tzu³ t'u¹	58	禿子禿
T'u¹ t'u¹ ch'a³	96	禿禿鋪
Tu³ li² 'r shu⁴	83	杜黎兒樹
Tung¹ yü⁴ miao⁴	56	東嶽廟
Tung¹ tung¹ tung¹	146	咚咚咚
Tsao⁴ uang² ye²	212	竈王爺
Tzu³ pu⁴ tzu³	159	紫不紫
Uo³ i¹ ko⁴ ta⁴ eur² tzu	15	我一個大兒子
Uo³ eur² tzu shuei⁴ chiao⁴ la	16	我兒子睡覺了
Uo³ ti¹ eur² no³ ti¹ chiao¹	182	我的兒我的姣

Ya¹ t'ou² ya¹	97	丫頭丫
Yang² shu⁴ ye⁴ 'r	6	楊樹葉兒
Yang² pa¹ pa¹ tan⁴ 'r	118	羊巴巴蛋兒
Yang³ huo² chu¹ ch'ih¹ k'ou³ jou⁴	197	養活豬吃口肉
Ye² ye² pao⁴ sun¹ tzu	106	爺爺抱孫子
Yen⁴ pien¹ hu²	129	簷蝙蝠
You³ ko⁴ niu¹ 'r pu⁴ hai⁴ sao¹	121	有個妞兒不害羞
You³ ko⁴ hsiao³ t'u¹ 'r	122	有個小禿兒本姓高
You³ pien¹ 'r you³ pien¹ 'r	144	有邊兒有邊兒
Yüe⁴ liang⁴ ye²	150	月亮爺
Yüe⁴ liang⁴ ye²	172	月亮爺
Yüe⁴ liang⁴ ye²	190	月亮爺

PEKING. — Pei-t'ang Press.

PEKINESE BABY-SONGS

I

鋸大拉
鋸大扯
頭木鋸
子房蓋
家姥姥
子娘娶

棚大搭
戲大唱
姑姑接
娘女請
婿外小
甥也你
　去

NOTES

Singing these words, the mother or any elder of the family takes the baby by the hands and pushes him for and backwards as if it was really the matter of drawing a saw. 姥姥家 lao³ lao³ chia¹, the family of the mother's mother. 娶娘子 ch'ü³ niang² tzŭ, goes to fetch the bride for her son, niang²-tzŭ is the name for a wife, and here it is used instead of 新姑娘 hsin¹-ku¹-niang², the real term for a bride. 搭大棚 ta¹-ta⁴-p'eng², they raise a large matshed. The chinese houses have not generally large rooms, therefore in marriage, death, anniversary, and other occasions in which many guests are to be invited, an additional matshed is raised in the court-yard. 大戲 tā-hsī, a play performed in the matshed by hired actors, an amusement much liked by the Chinese, but which only rich people can afford to have in their houses. 接姑娘請女婿 chie¹ ku¹-niang² ch'ing³ nü³-hsü⁴, the grandmother with her family invites on this marriage occasion her married daughters and their husbands. 外甥 uai⁴-sheng¹, is the name by which a sister's son is designed.

TRANSLATION

(People) draw the saw — pull the saw — saw the wood — build rooms — the grandmother and her family go to fetch the bride — a large matshed is raised — in which a play is performed — and they come to take home the married daughters — and to invite their husbands — small nephew — do you want also to go?

II

台轆轆上
台轆轆下
來倒茶媽媽張家
茶也香
酒也香

十駝叫麻噴小明甚紅裏灰對解把阿我瞧
八不麻愣了小姐兒甚麼轂頭鼠子南着煞到完家子南你
個動愣含着小小後車轆坐皮荷來車阿南了現餑檳你這
駱駝一花你車轎個銀包了門煞邊親成餑榔個
駝口褲別來白俏鼠小個兒你家兒就夾物厭
裳衣水腿惱到馬人掛兒等阿那親我老茶瓣兒的老包牙
　　　　　　　　　拉家去　　　　　　飯

NOTES

軲轆台 ku¹ lu¹ t'ai²; a rounded stone placed Some times outside the outerdoors to sit on. 麻愣 ma²-leng⁴ is the dragon fly (libellula virgo); it ought to be correctly written 螞螂 and pronounced ma¹-lang², I have however preferred the more popular and incorrect form as the sounds and the tones of the characters correspond to the Pekinese pronunciation, and the correct form is popularly unknown. 含着 hen²-cho, holding something in the mouth without showing it. The correct pronunciation of the character 含 is han², as it is also pronounced in vulgar phrases as for instance 暗含着 an⁴ han² cho, hiddenly, without showing, said sometimes of a meaning hidden in words which pretend not to say anything. 褲腿 k'u⁴ t'uei³, cloth-bands wrapped around the ankles of ladies with small feet. 轎車 chiao⁴ ch'o¹, sort of cart longer than the ordinary one, used only by the upper mandarin classes. 俏人家 ch'iao⁴ jen² chia¹, a beautiful woman. 灰鼠 huei¹-shu³, the grey squirrel. 皮襖 p'i²-ao³, chinese overcoat lined with fur. 銀鼠 yin²-shu³, the white squirrel. 對子 tuei⁴-tzu, a pair; the numeral — one is wanting. 荷包 ho²-pao¹, a small side-pouch in which the chinese keep banknotes, or even betel-nuts. 小針兒 hsiao³-chen¹-eur, a small needle used by women to work flowers on a cloth. This working different from the embroidery is called 扎 cha¹. 轄 hsia¹, the character ought to be pronounced in the second tone, but here is pronounced in the first because it is only used to represent the Manchu word *hiyà* meaning a body-guard of the sovereign; this word is very often used in Peking instead of the chinese equivalent 侍衛 shih⁴-wei⁴. 阿煞 a¹-sha¹, two characters which represent the Manchu word *asha* meaning one's elder brother's wife, and is used in the same complimentary way and in the same meaning as the chinese 嫂子 sao³-tzŭ. 達子餑餑 ta²-tzŭ puo¹-puo¹, tartar-cakes many of which keep yet their old Manchu names, and are largely used in Peking. 奶茶 nai³-ch'a², "milk-tea". 安南檳榔 an¹-nan²-ping¹-lang², Annamite betel-nuts. 夾四瓣兒 chia¹-ssu⁴-pan⁴'r, which are cut in four pieces. 硌 ko⁴ character not mentioned in any dictionary; it means to stick in the teeth, and also to hinder, to hurt. 厭物兒 yen⁴ u⁴'r, despising term for a person who disgusts people; it could be translated " you worrying thing!" 包牙 pao¹ ya², it is said of the front teeth when they protrude under the upper lip.

TRANSLATION

Goes up the sitting-stone — comes down from the sitting stone (!). The old lady Chang comes to pour tea — the tea is fragrant — the wine is fragrant — ten camels are loaden with clothes — they are unable to move on — and they call the dragon-fly — the dragon fly-with the mouth full of water — spurts the young lady's figured ankle-bands — young lady, young lady do not get cross — to-morrow or after to-morrow the cart shall arrive — what cart? — a chair-cart with red wheels, drawn by a white horse — and inside there sits a beautiful woman — who wears an over coat lined with grey squirrel fur and a jacket lined with ermine fur — and has with her a pair of side-pouches with flowers worked on it by the small needle — then, comes from the south direction an Imperial body-guard of the second class — who leaning to the cart-door asks his sister-in-law — sister-in-law, sister-in law, where do you go? — "I am going towards South to pay a visit to my family" — "When you have already paid a visit to your family, come to my house. — I have at home ready-cooked old rice — tartar cakes and tea milk — but the Annamite betel-nuts cut in four pieces — shall break the protruding old front teeth of you worrying thing!"

III

楊 樹 葉 兒
嘩 拉 拉
小 孩 兒 睡 覺 找 他 媽
乖 乖 寶 貝 兒 你 睡 罷
螞 虎 子 來 了 我 打 他

NOTES

楊樹 yang² shu⁴, the poplar (latin *populus*) this tree is in China very commonly seen in burial grounds. The Chinese say that its leaves stir even without wind, and that the noise produced by their stirring, moves to sadness. 嘩拉拉 hua¹ la¹ la¹, pronounced as one word, is imitative of the noise. This sad introduction is supposed to scare the boy and to get him sooner asleep. 乖乖 kuai¹-kuai¹, means to kiss as chinese mothers kiss their children in somewat a different way than the Europeans. The same expression is used too to say: be quiet! dont be saucy! — probably the two meanings melt in one, as the second may simply be a promise of a kiss if the boy will be quiet. Another common form for the last meaning is adverbially formed so, 乖乖兒的 kuai⁴ kuai⁴'r ti. 螞虎子 ma¹ hu³ tzŭ, a phantastic monstruos creature spoken of and called every time it is thought proper to scare a baby.

TRANSLATION

The poplar leaves — are stirring — the baby is about to sleep and looks for his mother — be a good boy, my treasure, get asleep — if the bogie comes, I'll beat him.

IV

挑水的哥
聽着我說
南河沿兒

有 你 的 窩
晴 天 晒 蓋 子
陰 天 把 脖 兒 縮

NOTES

These words are adressed by the chinese boys to the water-carriers who are generally people of the Shantung province. As no water-ways of any kind exist in Peking, a great many of these fellows take the water from the wells into the houses. Their bad pronunciation, and their awkward manners delight extremely the Peking cockneys. The boys have therefore composed for their benefit this special song, which they hum at their back, and whose general aim is to define them as turtles. The word turtle in China is used for one of the most direst insults, as this animal is phantastically empeached of an unnatural crime. The insult is however so largely used that people are not shocked by it. 哥 ko¹ means elder brother, but here is used in the meaning of man, fellow in the same way as the Russians use the word brat (latin *frater*). 窩 uo¹ means not only a nest but also a den, a hole. 晒蓋子 shai⁴ kai⁴- tzŭ, to dry the shell in the run, as turtles do. 縮 suo¹, to withdraw one's head, to retreat. This last phrase is allusive to the fact that the water-carriers do not go out when it rains, as the turles do too.

TRANSLATION

Water carrying fellow — hear what I say — on the bank of the south river — is your hole — when the weather is fine, you dry out your shell — and when it is bad weather then you draw in your neck.

V

沙土地兒
跑白馬
一跑跑到丈人家
大舅兒望裏讓
小舅兒望裏拉
隔着竹簾兒看見他
銀盤大臉黑頭髮
月白緞子棉襖銀疙疸

NOTES

沙土地兒 sha¹ t'u³ ti⁴'r, a sandy plain ground as outside the wall between the Manchu and the Chinese town in Peking. 丈人 chang⁴-jen, name given to one's wife or bride's father. 大舅兒 ta⁴-chiou⁴'r, one's wife's elder brother. 小舅兒 hsiao³ chiou⁴'r, one's wife's younger brother. For 他 is here to be understood the bride whom the young man succeeds in spying through the curtain. 銀盤大

臉 yin² p'an² ta⁴ lien³, a big face as white as a silver tray. 月白 yüe⁴ pai², "moon white" means a light blue. 疙疸 read kɔ¹-ta¹ or more vulgarly ka¹-ta¹, here means a metal button, it may also mean pimples and has other different shades of meanings.

TRANSLATION

On the sandy plain — gallops a white horse — galloping gets to the (horseman's) future father-in-law's house — his elder brother-in-law invites him to come in — his younger brother-in-law pulls him in — through the bamboo-curtain he has seen her — her large face as white as a silver-tray and her black hair — and her cotton overcoat of light azure colour with silver buttons.

VI

兒咧咧
禿咧咧
小咧咧
爹是你爹
你爹戴着紅纓帽
你媽穿着乍板兒鞋
南邊兒打水
走一步
蹋拉拉
十個脚指頭露着三

NOTES

The chinese boys generally as far as three years old have their hair shaven; therefore a common nickname for a boy is 禿兒 t'u¹'r, meaning a bald-headed. 咧咧咧 lie⁴-lie⁴-lie⁴, is imitative of the sound of weeping. The boy weeps and to quiet him the song is sung to him. 打水 ta³ shuei³, to draw water from a well, by a rope and a bucket. 紅纓子 hung² ing¹ tzǔ, Red silk twists fixed round the top of a chinese official hat. 乍板兒鞋 cha⁴ pan³'r hsie², old shoes with no heels; they are so called because the noise the sole produces slapping on the ground is like the sound of a chinese musical instrument called 乍板兒 cha⁴ pan³'r, consisting in two small bamboo tablets strung together, which are shaken by the fingers in a similar manner to the spanish and italian castanets 踢拉拉 t'a¹ la¹ la¹, imitates the slapping of the shoe sole on the ground. 三 san¹ is here (as very often in vulgar language) pronounced sa¹, in order to rhyme with the precedent verse who ends with 拉.

TRANSLATION

Small bald-headed — here he is weeping! — to the South side it's your father who draws water from the well — your father wears an official hat with red silk twists on it — and your mother wears on her feet old shoes with no heels — as she advances a step — it sounds t'alalà — and of her ten toes three peep out of her shoes.

VII

痲爬咬拿痲錢買了個痲燒餅吃

痲于樹叉叉的大了個痲燒餅吃

痲上狗人嚇痲買痲子看痲子打架痲子勸

子摔了個痲跟頭

痲子打架痲子勸

痲衙役

拿板子

單打痲子的痲腿子

NOTES

This song is profusedly interspersed with the character 痲 ma² whose meaning is "small pox." This disease is so common in China that very often children who have been sick with it and keep marks on their faces are familiarly called 痲子 ma²-tzŭ. Furthermore the word is used in other relative meanings. Here throughout these words, it is impossible to translate it always, as the repetition is done for the sake of playing on the word. The character I have written here is the regular one, but popularly the other character 麻 ma², which means hemp, is substituted for it. In the first verse it is repeated to intensify the original meaning, thus saying "much marked with small pox." 痲跟頭 ma² ken¹ t'ou², ken¹-t'ou² is a tumble; the word 痲 ma² is referred to the subject. 痲大錢 ma² ta⁴ ch'ien², so is called a cash when its surface is sugged, uneven, as if there were marks of small pox on it. 痲燒餅 ma² shao¹ ping³, a wheaten cake with an uneven surface, as it is when sesamum seeds are placed on it. 燒餅 shao¹ ping³, round wheaten cake.

TRANSLATION

The boy much marked with the small pox — climbs up a tree — the dog barks — and people go to catch him. — The small-pox marked is so scared that he tumbles. — With an old rugged cash he buys a cake — a small pox marked eats — and a small pox marked looks on — the small pox marked come to a fight — and a small-pox marked advises peace — small pox marked policemen — take the bamboo stick — and only thrash the legs of the small pox marked boy.

VIII

兒兒燒
頑兒燒瓜苦豆腐爛雞蛋
我鎌兒甜瓜豆腐雞蛋頭坐出坐出鼻
跟火鎌甜瓜豆腐雞蛋頭哥頭奶了
誰打火賣甜賣豆茶雞裏哥裏奶燒

殼哥哥買茶奶香睛
殼哥哥買奶燒眼
蛋着來着來子

NOTES

火鎌兒 huo³ lien²'r, a piece of steel used to strike sparks from a flint.　甜瓜 t'ien² kua¹, sweet melon.　豆腐 tou⁴-fu³, bean cheese, largely used in China　茶雞蛋 ch'a² chi¹ tan⁴, eggs boiled in tea.　雞蛋殼兒 chi¹ tan⁴ k'o¹'r the shell of an egg; it is generally pronounced k'o²'r.

TRANSLATION

Who is going to play with me? — strike the flint-steel — the flint steel takes fire — sell sweet melons — the sweet melons are bitter — sell bean cheese — the bean cheese is spoiled — boil eggs in tea — in the shell of the egg, of the egg — there is sitting the elder brother — the elder brother goes out to buy provisions — inside there sits the grand-mother — the grand mother goes out to burn incense — and burns her nose and her eyes.

IX

我 一 個 大 兒 子
一 個 兒 子
寶 貝 疙 疸 兒
開 胸 順 氣 丸

NOTES

These words are often repeated by the pekinese mothers to their babies 疙疸兒 ko¹ ta¹ 'r, means here a little thing of a round form just as it was a round metal button. 開胸順氣丸 k'ai¹ hsiung¹ shun⁴ ch'i⁴ uan², is a medical pill advised by chinese doctors to people who feel the breast oppressed and the respiration uneasy. The literal translation of its name is "pill which opens (lightens) the breast and makes the respiration easy. The mothers liken their babies to that pill, and really every mother holding her child in her arms must feel happy and free from every sorrow.

TRANSLATION.

This one great son of mine! — one son of mine! a precious little thing! — a pill who lightens the heart and makes people happy!

X

我兒子睡覺了
我花兒困覺了
我花兒把卜了
我花兒是個乖兒子
我花兒是個哄人精

NOTES

These words are repeated by mothers near the cradles of their sons to get them asleep. The phrase 把卜了 pa⁴ pu³ la, is rather difficult to explain, because the Chinese themselves cannot give it a meaning. However, after many enquiries I see that people are generally of opinion that this phrase has the meaning of being drowsy, being asleep. 乖兒子 kuai¹ eur² tzǔ, an obedient boy, meaning derived from the above mentioned phrase 乖乖 kuai¹ kuai¹, "be quiet!" 哄人的精 hung³ jen² ti ching¹, the word hung³ which means commonly to deceive, but its original meaning is to cajole, to flatter, to charm. The word ching¹ means essence, semen; the whole phrase could be translated: the essence, the flower of those who charm people.

TRANSLATION

My flower is sleeping — my flower has fallen asleep — my flower is resting — my flower is a quiet son — my flower is the flower of those who charm people.

XI

家花了家擀麪片
看梅探探我會擀大片
你邊探沒到兒一
狗花兒如線
黃南梅人媳擀麪賽團團轉
狗到朵梅人媳擀麪刀在鍋裏蓮花瓣
黃我一雙我家起起擱在鍋裏
拿拿擱盛在碗裏

碗半碗眼瞪瞪的睡

一碗兩碗碗碗瞪在那兒睡

婆兒藏起來了上直兒婦媳睡

一碗下來舔砸鋸兒婦媳

婆姑下來舔婦媳裏

一個小底過過過媳兒坑甚麼皮甚麼皮錘

公兩案貓狗耗嚇媳在鋪鋪蓋蓋枕枕公公拿着一落磚婆婆拿着一溜鞭打的媳婦兒一溜烟

NOTES

This song although very childish, yet is founded on the fact that chinese mothers-in-law are often unkind and sometimes even cruel to their daughters-in-law. 雙雙人兒 shuang¹ shuang¹ jen²ʳ, means a couple of persons, not four persons. 我家媳婦兒 uo³ chia¹ hsi² fu⁰ʳ, "the wife in my house" probably these words are meant to be uttered by the mother in law, who may call so her son's daughter. 擀麭 kan³ mien⁴, to stretch out dough to make vermicelli. 擀麭杖 kan³ mien⁴ chang⁴, a roller to stretch dough. 一大片 i¹ ta⁴ p'ien⁴, a large flat piece (of dough); in the text the verb "she stretches out" is wanting. 賽如線 sai⁴ ju⁴ hsien⁴, which may rival, compete with thread as to thinness. 團團轉 t'uan² t'uan² chuan⁴, conglomerated they turn round in the pan. (said of the vermicelli) 蓮花瓣 lien²-hua¹-pan⁴, (as they were) petals of the lotus blossom. 公 kung¹ father-in-law, here kung¹ is instead of 公公 kung¹ kung¹. 婆 p'uo², mother in law, here p'uo² is instead of 婆婆 p'uo² p'uo². 小姑兒 hsiao³ ku¹'r, her husband's younger sisters. 案板 an⁴ pan³, a wood board on which dough is stretched to make vermicelli. 爐坑 lu² k'eng¹ is a pit under the stove where the ashes fall down; an imcommon severe punishment inflicted by mothers-in-law to their daughters-in-law is to let them sleep in the stove-pit. 鋪甚麼 p'u¹ she² mmo, what have you for bedding? 枕甚麼 chen³ she² mmo, what have you for pillow? Somebody is supposed to ask now from the unfortunate wife about her condition. 棒錘 pang⁴ ch'ui², a beater used in washing clothes; it is generally made of 棗木 tsao³ mu⁴, date wood. 一落磚 i¹ luo⁴ chuan¹, a pile of bricks, that is to say, as many bricks as could form a pile of them. 一溜鞭 i¹ liou⁴ pien¹, "a row of whips" rather a strange expression for many whips, lots of whips. 一溜烟 i¹ liou⁴ yen¹, as a stream of smoke; the verse is not complete because its whole meaning is: they beat the wife so that she runs away as quickly as a stream of smoke (a cloud of smoke). The Chinese associate the idea of smoke with quickness; very often it is heard 他走一溜烟兒似的 t'a¹ tsou³ i¹ liou⁴ yen¹'r shih⁴-ti, he walks as quickly as a stream of smoke.

TRANSLATION

Yellow dog, yellow dog, look after the house — I go towards South to pluck plum-blossoms — I have not yet plucked a single plum-blossom — and two persons arrive at the house — my son's wife knows how to stretch out dough — she takes the roller and stretches a large slice of dough — she takes the knife and cuts vermicelli as thin as thread — then she puts them in the cooking-pan, and they turn conglomerated about — afterwards she puts them down in the bowls and they look like petals of the lotus blossom. — (She fills) one bowl for her father-in-law — one bowl for her mother-in-law — and two half-bowls for her sisters-in-law — she hides one bowl under the dough-board — but the cat comes over and licks the bowl — the dog comes over and has broken the bowl — the mice come over and gnaw the bowl — and the housewife is so scared that she stares vacantly — "wife, wife, where do you sleep?" — "I sleep in the stove-pit — what have you for bedding? — I have for bedding a goat's skin — what have you for coverlet? — I have a dog's skin — what have you for pillow? — I have a linen-beater — the father-in-law takes up in his hands as many bricks as could form a pile — the mother-in-law holds up in her hands a row of whips — and they beat the wife so that she runs away as quickly as a stream of smoke.

XII

寒鴉兒寒鴉兒過
一遍打十個
熬着吃
煑着吃
剝了皮兒更好吃

NOTES

寒鴉兒 han² ya¹'r' is the Corvus monedula, a white breasted crow; a large number of them comes to Peking from the North, at the beginning of winter, and their first apparition is greeted by the Pekinese boys with these verses who are however too gastronomic to be sentimental. The flesh of these crows is eatable, but the taste for it is not general. — 遍 i¹ pien⁴, at one time. 剝 puo¹ is read vulgarly pao².

TRANSLATION

The white breasted crows, the white breasted crows are passing — at one time we strike ten of them — we eat them boiled in gravy — we eat them boiled — but they are even better to eat when the skin is taken off them.

XIII

小白菜兒
地裏黃兒
七八歲沒了娘
好好兒跟着爹爹過
又怕爹爹娶後娘
娶了後娘三年整
養了個兄弟比我強
他吃菜
我泡湯
哭哭啼啼想親娘

NOTES

Of all the popular songs that are in this collection, I think this one could claim any artistic value. It is very simple, subject and words, but the child's grief is movingly depicted. The boy likenes himself to a small cabbage which gets yellow and dry in the earth, because nobody takes care of it. The comparison is not poetical for us, but in China there is nothing peculiarly vulgar attached to the word cabbage. 過 kuo⁴ is here for 過日子 kuo⁴ jih⁴-tzŭ, to live, to get on. 三年整 san¹ nien² cheng³, just after three years. 泡湯 p'ao⁴ t'ang¹, to pour the gravy on the rice. 哭哭啼啼 k'u¹ k'u¹ t'i² t'i², weeping and wailing.

TRANSLATION

Like the small cabbage — which has become yellow and dry on the ground — at the age of seven or eight years, I have lost my mother. — I lived so well near my father — only I was afraid he would take another wife — and he has taken her; just after three years — they have given me a brother who is more worthy than I am — because he eats the food — and I only may pour the gravy on my rice — weeping and wailing I think of my own mother!

XIV

張大嫂
李大嫂

坡角疼跑蓆草個保大饅
南豆子家炕炕了豆保開頭
上摘肚往撩鋪養叫豆又賣
兒子
又賣麭

NOTES

大嫂 ta⁴ sao³, general appellation for the eldest brother's wife; married women call each other ta⁴ sao³ for sake of ceremony. 豆角 tou⁴ chiao³, bean pods. 撩 liao¹, to grasp, to pull, here, "to pull away" 炕蓆 k'ang⁴ hsi², the mat wich is spread on the k'ang. Somebody could be curious to know which of the two ladies ran home, but the song does not satisfy the curiosity.

TRANSLATION

Mistress Chang — and Mistress Li — have gone to the Southern slope — to gather bean pods — (one of them) felt a pain in her bosom — and ran home — pulled off the k'ang-mat — spread dry grass on the k'ang — and bore a child whom she called Tou[1] pao[3] — Tou[1]-pao[3] not it has opened a shop — and sells bread and flower.

XV

日 頭 出 來 一 點 紅
師 傅 騎 馬 我 騎 龍
師 傅 騎 馬 遶 街 走
我 騎 青 龍 過 海 東
海 東 有 我 家
我 家 種 着 五 盆 花
大 姐 愛 個 紅 芍 藥
二 姐 愛 個 牡 丹 花
三 姐 愛 的 是 桃 花 瓣
四 姐 愛 的 是 大 蓮 花
剩 下 五 姐 無 的 愛
一 心 要 出 家
出 家 人 兒 樂 陶 陶
一 來 不 受 公 婆 氣
二 來 不 受 丈 夫 熬
三 來 懷 中 不 抱 子
四 來 散 淡 又 逍 遙

NOTES

芍藥 shao[2] yao[4], peony, lat. *pæonia* 牡丹 mu[3] tan[1].

the tree peony, lat. *pæonia mutan*. 蓮花, lien² hua¹, the lotus flower, lat. *Nelumbium speciosum*. 無的愛 u² ti¹ ai⁴, she has nothing that she likes. 出家 ch'u¹ chia¹, "to go out of the family" means to enter the monastic life. 樂陶陶 lo⁴ t'ao² t'ao², joyfully, happily. 熬 ao¹, to boil, to decoct, and figurately to vex, to disturb. 散淡 san³ tan⁴, freely, easily, with no coercions 逍遙 hsiao¹ yao², in a state of peace and bliss.

TRANSLATION

The sun has come out like a red spot — my teacher rides on a horse and I ride on a dragon — the teacher riding on the horse goes along the streets — I riding on the dark dragon cross over to the East of the sea — at the East of the sea there lives my family — and in my family they cultivate five fllower-pots — my first sister likes the red peony — my second sister likes the tree peony — my third sister likes the petals of the peach blossom — my fourth sister likes the large lotus blossoms. — There is the fifth sister who has nothing she may like — and does not think of other but of becoming a nun — the women in the monastic life live very happily indeed — firstly they do not suffer the vexations of father-and mother-in-law — secondly they do not suffer a husband's maltreatment — thirdly they do not bear children — and fourthly they live freely and in a condition of blissful peace.

XVI

剔 燈 棍 兒
打 燈 花 兒
爺 爺 兒 尋 了 個 禿 奶 奶 兒
眼 又 斜
嘴 又 歪
氣 的 爺 爺 兒 竟 發 獃

NOTES

剔燈棍兒 t'i teng¹ kun¹ 'r, a wire to pull up the wick in an oil lamp. 打燈花兒 ta³ teng¹ hua¹ 'r, to take away the burned part of the wick. — The scene depicted is rather a comic one; a man has married a woman whom he has never seen, and as soon as he enters the nuptial room, he snuffs the candle to see better and perceives that the bride is a very ugly one. 爺爺兒 ye² ye² 'r, means in vulgar Pekinese a man, a husband as 奶奶兒 nai³ nai³ 'r, means a woman, a wife. Both words are used in different meanings in family relations technology. 發獃 fa¹ tai¹, to stare vacantly.

TRANSLATION

With the oil-lamp wire — he takes away the burned wick — the man perceives he has got for himself a bald wife — she is squint eyed — and has a crooked mouth — the husband is so struck with anger — that he stares stupidity.

XVII

嚷地進了房
嚷地掃走　　香香地
姐郎的帳子　頭　鬧來娘　兒兒　長掃香
的的床　　　枕　海棠姑　花瓣禳地來花
的的被子　　鏡　香簪花紅落兒合
兒兒的褥子　花玉桃大拖花百尖圓
花花兒海棠　件　裙松起兒兒
花花兒菊兒花桂粉唇一羅聲掃花姑花
花花兒秋人銀頭官朱穿地了葉花葉
芝藥球聲美對油擦點身
茉莉蓉花芝藥球叫虞美兩梳臉嘴
石榴茉芙繡蘭芍綉叫虞兩梳臉嘴下叫松茨荷

靈芝開花兒抱牡丹
水仙開花兒香十里
梔子開花兒嫂嫂望江南

NOTES

It appears this song has no other aim than to put together the greatest number of flowers and plants names. 石榴花 shih² liu² hua¹, pomegranate flowers. 茉莉花 muo⁴ li⁴ hua¹, Arabian jasmine (lat. *Jasminum Sambœ*). 芙蓉花 fu¹ jung² hua¹, the Hibiscus mutabilis. 繡花 hsiou⁴ hua¹, flowers embroidered by hand. 蘭芝花 lan² chih¹ hua¹, and also 蘭花 lan² hua¹, the Cymbidium ensifolium. 綉球花 hsiou⁴ ch'iu¹ hua¹, sort of geranium (lat. *geranium zonale*). 鬧嚷嚷 nao⁴ jang¹ jang¹, to be noisy, here perhaps to be in confusion, to be meddled together. 秋菊 ch'iu¹ chü², autumn chrysanthemum. 海棠 hai³ t'ang², pyrus spectabilis, cultivated for its flowers and fruits. 虞美人 yü² mei² jen². papaver rhoeas, a double variety of the poppy. 桂花 kuei⁴ hua¹, the Cassia flower (lat. *Cinnamomum Cassia*). 官粉 kuan¹ fen³, sort of good white cosmetic powder which ladies rub on their cheeks 玉簪花 yü⁴ tsan¹ hua¹, Funkia subcordata. 下地 hsia⁴-ti⁴, to reach the ground. 羅裙 luo² ch'ün², a long petticoat, made with a sort of silk called 羅 luo². 拖落 t'uo¹ lo⁴, is said of the dresses when they are too long and the skirts sweep the ground. 松花 sung¹ hua¹, pine-flower. The Chinese use to throw the flowers into the stove to prevent the bad smell of coal. 百合花 pae³-ho²-hua¹ read also puo⁴-ho²-hua¹, the lily (lat. *Lilium*). 茨姑 tz'u² ku¹, an herb with arrowlike leaves (lat. *Sagittaria sagittifolia*). 荷花 ho² hua¹, the Lotus blossom, the same as 蓮花 lien² hua¹, (lat. *Nelumbium speciosum*). 靈芝 ling² chih¹, the plant of long life. 水仙 shuei³ hsien¹, the narcissus. 栀子 chih¹-tzŭ, the gardenia 望江南 uang⁴ chiang¹ nan², means literally " looking towards the South of the river " but it is also a flower name.

TRANSLATION

The bride, is the pomegranate flower — the bridegroom is the jasmin — the curtains are covered with flowers of the Hibiscus mutabilis — the bed is covered with embroidered flowers — the pillow is covered with flowers of Cymbidium ensifolium — and the coverlet is spread with peony flowers — the mattress is strown with geraniums flowers, which are in disorder — they call the autumn chrysanthemum and the flower of the pyrus spectabilis, to let them sweep the floor — here miss poppy has entered the room — there are two mirrors with frames inlaid with silver — and she combs her hair as perfumed as the Cassia flower — then she rubs her face with white cosmetic powder, with the smell of the Funkia subcordata — and she marks a red spot on her lips, as scented as petals of the peach blossom —

she wears a big red overcoat — and a petticoat so long that it sweeps the ground — then she calls the pine flower that it may sweep the floor — the pine flowers beegins to sweep the floor and a lily odour is smelt — the leaves of the Sagittaria sagittifolia are pointed — the leaves of the lotus blossom are round — the plant of immortality opening the flowers embraces the tree peony — the narcissus opens the flowers and the odour is smelt as far as ten lî — the gardenia opens the flowers and the sister-in-law " looks toward South."

XVIII

槐樹槐
槐樹底下搭戲台
人家的姑娘都來了
我家的姑娘還不來
說着說着就來了
騎着驢
打着傘
光着脊梁挽着纂

NOTES

槐樹 huai² shu⁴, the ash tree (lat. *fraxinus*). 打着傘 ta³ cho¹ san³, keeping the umbrella open. 光着脊梁 kuang¹ cho¹ chi³ niang³, bare from head to waist. 挽着纂 uan³ cho¹ tsuan³, with the back-hair combed as a chignon.

TRANSLATION

Ash trees, ash trees — under the ash trees they have raised a stage — everybody's girls are come — only mine does not come yet — just while speaking, here she is come — riding on a donkey — with an open parasol — and with her hair combed into a chignon.

XIX

哥兒多飯
二飯兒了老婆
小吃吃完打
打的老婆上窗戶
窗戶沒有檔兒
打的老婆照鏡兒
鏡子沒有底兒
打的老婆唱曲兒
曲兒沒有頭兒
打的老婆要猴兒
猴兒沒有圈兒
打的老婆鑽天兒

NOTES

There is not much coherence in the words, and the fun is in the fact that many verses are ended with the final 兒, which produces a ridiculous effect. 二哥 eur⁴ ko¹, the second brother in the family also simply a familiar name. 老婆 lao³ p'uo², an old woman, a wife. The accent falls generally on the 老 lao³ in this meaning; but if said lao³ p'uo² tzŭ³, with the accent on the p'uo², then it means "a female servant". 檔兒 tang⁴ 'r, small wood bars placed horizontally in the chinese window-sash. 耍猴兒 shua³ hou² 'r, "to (let) play the monkey, that is to exhibit the tricks of a monkey to gain the life"; the other metaphorical meaning is "to lark, to romp, to be impertinent". 圈兒 ch'iuan¹ 'r, a wooden circle through which the monkeys are let jump.

TRANSLATION

The small second brother — eats too much — and when he has finished eating — he beats his wife — and the wife is so beaten that she jumps on the window — the window has no bars — and the wife is so beaten that she looks in the mirror — the mirror has no bottom — the wife is beaten so that she begins to sing — the song has no end — the wife is so beaten that she "plays with the monkey" —

the monkey has no circle — and the wife is so beaten that she springs up to the sky.

XX

金轱轆棒
銀轱轆棒
爺爺兒打板兒
奶奶兒唱
一唱唱到大天亮
養活了個孩子沒處兒放
一放放在鍋台上
噝兒噝兒的喝米湯

NOTES

轱轆棒 ku¹ lu⁴ pang⁴, a child toy, consisting in a short wood mace with a handle. The wood above the handle is circularly worked as to give the idea of wheels 轱轆 ku¹ lu⁴. It is the imitation of an ancient chinese weapon. 大天亮 ta⁴ t'ien¹ liang⁴, when the daylight was very bright. 噝兒噝兒 tzŭ¹ 'r tzŭ¹ 'r, imitates the sound produced by the lips of a person who is sipping broth. There was no character in the dictionary for it, but I was forced to adopt the above written as corresponding to the exact sound and having by side the radical 口.

TRANSLATION

Gilt wood mace — silvered wood mace — the husband strikes the castanets and the wife sings — and they have been singing till broad daylight — and she has born a child, and there was no place to lay him — and they have laid him on the kitchen-stove — where he is sipping the rice gravy.

XXI

圓轆轆門前掛紅線

圓門厚袖甩在門後頭

扯軲家線大甩後腰刀尖天雷賊嘩拉又一回

扯扯家紅甩一門掛腰頂天狗唏嚕

NOTES

These words are sung by children as they give each other the hand and turn around in a circle: no particulary defined meaning is attached to them, as they are put together only to keep measure with the steps. 軲轆圓 ku¹ lu⁴ yüan², as round as a wheel. 甩 shuai³, expresses a movement peculiar to the Chinese, that of letting down with a sudden jerk of the arm, the long sleeve which was tucked up the wrist. 唏嚹嘩拉 hsi¹ liu¹ hua¹ la¹, words with no meaning.

TRANSLATION

Draw, draw — draw the circle as round as a wheel — at every house-door is hanging a red thread — the red thread is thick — drop the sleeve — drop it as far as behind the door — behing the door — is hanging the swoard — the swoard is cutting — and is so long that it touches the sky — the sky thunders — the dog bites the thieves — hsiliuhualà once more!

XXII

大禿子得病
二禿子慌

三禿子請大夫
四禿子熬薑湯
五禿子抬
六禿子埋
七禿子哭着走進來
八禿子問他哭甚麽
我家死了個禿乖乖
快快兒抬
快快兒埋
別讓那個葫蘆子兒迸出來

NOTES

For a baldhead is meant in this song a child, for the reason explained before. 薑湯 chiang¹ t'ang¹, ginger broth, a medicine given to make the patient sweat. 乖乖 kuai¹ kuai¹, dear, treasure, said of children. 葫蘆子兒 hu² lu² tzǔ³ 'r, the seeds in his gourd (meaning his head). 迸出來 peng⁴ ch'u¹ lai², to spring up; said of things which being thrown down, by force of elasticity, spring up.

TRANSLATION

The first baldhead gets sick — the second baldhead is scared — the third baldhead goes to call a doctor — the fourth baldhead boils a ginger decoction — the fifth baldhead bears him (the sick one) on the shoulders — the sixth baldhead buries him — the seventh baldhead comes in — the eight baldead asks "why do you weep"? — In my family a dear baldhead is dead — quickly take him away — quickly bury him — lest the seeds should spring out of his gourd.

XXIII

樹葉青
呀呀兒英
我跟姐姐過一冬
姐姐蓋着花花被睡
妹妹蓋着羊皮子襖
姐姐穿着紬子襖
妹妹穿着破皮襖
姐姐戴着金簪子
妹妹戴着竹圈子
姐姐騎着高頭馬
妹妹騎着樹喀杈
姐姐登着銀鐙兒
妹妹登着牆縫兒
姐姐抱着個銀娃娃
妹妹抱着個癩蛤蟆
走一步來哇兒呱哇兒呱又哇兒呱

NOTES

呀呀兒英 ya¹ ya¹ 'r ying¹, meaningless refrain which rhymes with the preceding verse. 花花被 hua¹ hua¹ pei⁴, a coverlet embroidered with flowers. 簪子, tsan¹ tzŭ, chinese hair-pin. 竹圈子 chu² ch'iüan¹ tzŭ, ear-rings made of bamboo; in Peking ear-rings are generally called 鉗子 ch'ien² tzŭ. 嘎杈 k'a¹ ch'a¹, a forked branch 癩蛤蟆 lai⁴ ha² ma¹, a scabby toad. 哇兒呱 ku¹ 'r kuà¹, imitates the voice of a toad.

TRANSLATION

The tree leaves are dark — I spend a winter with my elder sister — my elder sister covers her bed with a coverlet embroidered with flowers — and I the younger sister cover my bed with a goat skin — my elder sister wears a satin overcoat — I the younger sister wear a broken skin overcoat — my elder sister wears golden hair-pins — and I the younger sister wear bamboo ear-rings — my elder sister rides on a splendid horse — and I the younger sister ride on a forked branch — my elder sister leans her feet on silver stirrups — and I the younger sister lean my feet on the wall crevices — my elder sister holds in her arms a silver baby — and I the younger sister hold in my arms a scabby toad — which moves a step and then cries kurkuà kurkuà.

XXIV

立了秋來立了秋
八月十五月兒照高樓
鴉雀無聲人烟靜
瞧見了兩個押虎子走籌
一根燈草嫌他不亮
兩根燈草又怕費了油
有心要買一枝羊油燭
怎奈我手中沒有猴兒頭

NOTES

立秋 li⁴ ch'iu¹, the beginning of winter. 照 chao⁴, illumines. 人烟靜, jen² yen¹ ching⁴, men and smoke (houses) are resting; everything is quiet. 押虎子 ya¹ hu³ tzŭ, Peking street watchmen, kept by the Government to tell the hour by striking on a bamboo rattle. 走籌 tsou³ ch'ou², to take round by night time a bamboo tally from one watch-post to another. 一根燈草 i¹ ken¹ teng¹ ts'ao³, a lamp wick made of the stalk of the Juncus communis (rushes). 怎奈 tsen³ nai⁴, there is no remedy, no way. 猴兒頭 hou² 'r t'ou², a monkey's head, slang Pekinese term to mean money. Several words are used in the same meaning as for instance 大軲轆 ta⁴ ku¹ lu⁴, the big wheel. 官板 kuan¹ pan³, official stamp, stamped by the Government. Several terms cannot be written at all, wanting a character for them, not with standing I will venture to write them down with homophonous characters. So for instance 嘎, read ka². Ex. 我的這個褡連兒就剩了叫喚嘎了 no³ ti¹ che¹-ko⁴ ta¹-lien² 'r ciou⁴ sheng⁴ la chiao⁴ huan⁴ ka² la, "there is noting left in my purse but noisy cash" meaning that the purse only contains two or three cash which at every step meet and ring. It is also said 古嘎 ku³ ka². Ex. 古嘎沒有 ku³ ka² mei² iou³, I have no cash. Another term is 側 ts'o², or 側羅 ts'o² lo². Foreign words are sometimes used as chi¹-ha¹, the chinese transformation of the Manchu word *jiha* "money" and chao¹ su¹, said to be Mongol and generally used, peculiarly in the whole phrase chao¹ su¹ u¹ kuei³, which is meant for "I have no money" and is all in Mongol.

TRANSLATION

The autumn has set in, the autumn has set in — on the fifteenth of the eighth month the moon illumines the high palaces — crows and other birds are silent and men and houses are resting — I have seen two watchmen who went round taking the watch-tally — here, with only one wick in the lamp, I am sorry it is dark — but I am afraid to consume too much oil burning two wicks — I intend buying a candle of mutton-tallow — but, alas! I have not a single cash in the hands.

XXV

小五兒
小六兒
一塊冰糖兒
一包豆兒
小五兒愛吃糖兒
一爬爬到柳枝兒
小柳樹稍軟了
摔的小五兒直翻眼
小六兒愛上高樹稍
戴上鬍子唱戲
唱完了戲
唱熱湯不涼
湯燙的小六兒叫親娘

NOTES

Chinese children are given by their parents a 奶名 nai³ ming², "milk-name" by which they are designated in the family. These milk names are numberless. A common habit in the family is to give the new born children only a number for milk name, by which number the child is called *four* or *five*, if it is the fourth or fifth son in the family. The common forms for these arithmetical names are such: A first born may be called 一子 i¹-tzŭ, (the form is not much used; the accent falls on the i¹). The second son may be called 二哥 eur⁴ ko¹, or 小一兒 hsiao³ i¹ 'r. The third son may be called 三兒 san¹ 'r, the fourth 四兒 ssŭ⁴ 'r, the fifth 五兒 u³ 'r, the sixth 六兒 liou⁴ 'r, and so forth as far as ten. These milk names are also given to children independently of their order in the family and become like our christian names Charles, John and so forth. 氷糖 ping¹ t'ang², white sugar in pieces sold on the streets to children. 一包豆兒 i¹ pao¹ tou⁴ 'r, a parcel of roasted beans, another delicacy for children. 翻眼 fan¹ yen³, to turn up the eyes, like a man who loses his senses and shows the white of his eyes. 淘氣 t'ao²-ch'i⁴, impertinent, saucy. 戴上鬍子 tai⁴ shang⁴ hu² tzŭ, to put on a false beard as actors do in theaters.

TRANSLATION

The small Five — and the small Six — with a piece of white sugar — and a parcel of beans — the small Five likes to go high up — and he climbs up to the tip of the branch of the willow tree — the tip of the willow branch is weak — and the small Five tumbles down and hurts himself so that he shows the white of his eyes. — The small Six is really impertinent — he puts on a false beard and sings an act of an opera — when he has finished singing the opera, — he drinks hot broth — the broth is not cool — and the small Six scalds himself so that he calls for his mother.

XXVI

小小子兒
坐門礅兒
哭着喊着要媳婦兒
要了媳婦兒作甚麼
點上燈說話兒
吹了燈作伴兒
明兒個起來梳小辮兒

NOTES

門礅兒 men² tun¹ 'r, a big stone-seat placed by the side of a street door. 喊着 han³ cho, crying loudly.

TRANSLATION

The small boy — is sitting outside the door on the stone-seat — and weeping and wailing he wants to have a wife — when he has got a wife what will he do with her? — when the lamp is lighted he will have a chat with her — when then the lamp is out he will keep company wich her —

and the next morning after getting up she will comb his small pigtail.

XXVII

高 高 山 上 有 一 家
十 間 房 子 九 間 塌
老 頭 子 出 來 拄 拐 棍 兒
老 婆 子 出 來 就 地 兒 擦
看 家 的 狗 兒 三 條 腿
避 鼠 的 貍 貓 短 個 尾 巴

NOTES

拄 chu³, to lean on a stick. 拐棍兒 kuai³ kun⁴ 'r, a stick used by old men to lean on. 就地兒 chiou⁴ ti⁴ 'r, bent to the ground (walking) as very old men do. 擦 ts'a¹, to walk painfully dragging (rubbing) the feet on the ground. 避鼠的貓 pi⁴ shu³ ti¹-mao¹, a cat which shuns (does not catch) mice. 貍貓 li² mao¹, the wild cat.

TRANSLATION

On a very high mountain there lives a family — of the ten rooms in the building nine rooms are in ruin — the old man goes out leaning on a stick —

and the old wife walks painfully and bent to the ground. — the dog which watches the house has only three legs — the wild cat which does not catch the mice is without a tail.

XXVIII

香蒿子兒
香刺刺罐兒
香刺蔴兒
香菜兒
喇叭喇叭花兒
翠雀兒
買我的是好漢兒
買別人的是龜蓋兒喲

NOTES

These words are sung by Pekinese boys who want to imitate the ambulant grocer, and tell aloud the names of their wares. 香蒿子 hsiang¹ hao¹ tzŭ, the Artemisia annua-the chinese make with its dry stalks a sort of vegetable rope which they burn to keep away mosquitoes. 刺刺罐兒 la¹ la¹ kuan⁴ 'r, a wild grass which grows at the beginning of spring. 苦蕒兒 or 苦菜 k'u³ ts'ai⁴, the sowthistle (lat. *Lonchus arvensis*). 香菜 hsiang¹ ts'ai⁴, "odorous herbs" (lat. *Coriandrum sativum*) the chinese use its leaves for parsley. 喇叭花 la³ pa¹ hua¹, "trumpet flowers" is the white stramony (lat. *Datura alba*). 翠雀兒 ts'uei⁴ ch'iao³ 'r, the larkspur (lat. *Delfinium anthriscifolium*). 龜蓋兒 kuei¹ kai⁴ 'r, a mild form of the common chinese insult "turtle-shell".

TRANSLATION

Here is Artemisia annua — here is lalaqua'r grass — here are sowthistle and parsley — white stramony flowers — and larkspur — who buys my ware is a good fellow — and who buys other people's is a "turtle-shell".

XXIX

泥泥泥泥餑餑
泥泥泥泥人兒
老頭兒喝酒不讓人兒
買我的是個好漢兒
不買我的是個王八蛋兒

NOTES

Chinese boys are till a certain age as busy in the manufacture of mud-pies as any other boy in foreign countries. They buy for a few cash ready-made moulds out of which they work pagodas, small fishes, turtles, and so forth. When the wares are ready and dry, the small merchants sing these verses as if they meant to sell the products of their work. 泥餑餑 ni² puo¹ puo¹, is the exact equivalent of the english "mud-pie".

TRANSLATION

Here are mud pies — here are mud figures — the old man drinks wine and does not offer to others — who buys my ware is a good fellow — and who does not buy mine is a turtle's egg.

XXX

水牛兒水牛兒
先出觭角後出頭
你爹你媽
給你買下燒肝兒燒羊肉

NOTES

In all countries children have verses to address snails, and in China too, although the meaning of the verses is not to be looked for. 水牛兒 shuei³ niu² 'r, the snail.

TRANSLATION

Snail, snail — you first show out your horns and

then your head — your father and mother — will buy for you some roasted liver and roasted mutton.

XXXI

妞兒要吃麪叚兒
給你找老細兒來　兒不哼哎喲
寬條棍兒
簾子
妞兒要吃肉六
給你找老後腿兒來　兒不哼哎喲
腰窩瘦
篔肥兒
妞兒要吃梨糕
還得冰糖熬呀
篔酥呀一個脆
好大的　塊兒呀哼哎喲
妞兒要喝豆汁兒
還得找老西兒的
酸酸黃瓜菜辣兒的
酸兒　辣兒來不哼哎喲
妞兒要吃白薯
給你找老五大塊兒
黃穰兒的
栗子味兒呀哼哎喲

NOTES

妞兒 niu¹ 'r, girl, familiar term for 姑娘 ku¹ niang². 吃麪 ch'ih¹ mien⁴, to eat vermicelli. 麪 mien⁴ is here for 麪條兒 mien¹ t'iao² 'r, 老叚 Laô³ tuan⁴, the old man named Tuan, probably a shop-keeper. 寬條兒 k'uan¹ t'iao² 'r, flat and large vermicelli. 細條兒 hsi⁴ t'iao² 'r, finer vermicelli. 簾子棍兒 lien²-tzŭ³ kun⁴ 'r, another sort of vermicelli so called because of its resemblance to the bamboo sticks which are bound together to form a summer curtain. 來不哼哎喲 lai² pu eng a-yo, meaningless refrain. 腰窩兒 iao¹ uo¹ 'r, "the loins nest" the best part of the loins of a mutton or a beef. 後腿兒 hou⁴ t'uei³ 'r, the back part of the thigh. 眞肥瘦 chen¹ fei² shou⁴, "really there are both fat and lean", that is very good meat-a buyer going to the butcher's shop, if not particularly wishing to get more fat or more lean, calls the meat he wants 肥瘦 fei² shou⁴ that is fat and lean together. So the phrase 你給我一斤肥瘦兒 ni³ kei³ uo³ i¹ chin¹ fei² shou⁴ 'r, means "give me a pound of good meat". 棃糕 li² kao¹, pear jam dried in slices. 酥 su¹, is said of the food and particularly of pastry, when it is so delicate that it melts in the mouth-french "fondant". 脆 ts'uei⁴, crisp. 豆汁兒 tou⁴ chih¹ 'r, a decoction of seeds which is drunk in spring time and is thought a powerful agent to cool one's blood: it is mostly used by Bannermen. 老西兒 lao³ hsi¹ 'r, nickname given by the Pekinese to the natives of the Shan-hsi province, who do not enjoy a very good reputation, even among Pekinese. Here they are quoted because they are generally fond of sour food as the tou⁴-chih¹ is. 黃瓜菜 huang² kua¹ ts'ai⁴, salted cucumber. 白薯 pae² shu³, the sweet potatoes. 瓤兒 jang² 'r, the pulp of a fruit, the stuff of a pudding, generally the interior of objects, from a cake to a clock.

TRANSLATION

Young lady, if you want to eat vermicelli, — we will go to see the old Tuan for you, — who has flat vermicelli, and thin vermicelli — and " curtain-sticks " vermicelli — Young lady, if you want to eat meat — we will go to the old Six's for you — he has got good loin of mutton and good haunch of mutton — both fat and lean meat — Young lady, if you want to eat pear-jam — we must also boil it in white sugar — it is really melting in the mouth and so crisp! — and what a big slice of it! — Young lady, if you want to drink bean decoction — then we must go to the old Shan-hsi man's — how sour it is! how bitter it is! — and how sour the salt cucumbers taken with it — Young lady, if you want to eat sweet potatoes — we will go to the old Five's — who has there large slices of sweet potato pulp — which smell like chestnuts.

XXXII

出 了 門 兒
陰 了 天 兒
抱 着 肩 兒
進 茶 館 兒
靠 爐 台 兒
找 個 朋 友 尋 倆 錢 兒
出 茶 館 兒
飛 雪 花 兒
老 天 爺
竟 和 窮 人 鬧 着 頑 兒

NOTES

These verses are supposed to be uttered by a beggar who complains of his bad luck on a winter's day. The song is rhymed by adding the character 兒 **eur**^{2} at the end of each verse. 抱着肩兒 **pao**^{4} **cho**^{2} **chien**^{1} **'r**, lit. "embracing one's shoulder" that is to keep the arms folded on the breast, as chinese beggars do when they feel cold. 爐台兒 **lu**^{2} **t'ai**^{2} **'r**, a small stove made of bricks. 尋 **hsin**^{2}, means to ask something from somebody, to look for, the ordinary sound of the character is hsün. 老天爺 **lao**^{3} **t'ien**^{1} **ye**^{2}, the old gentleman in the sky. Has no relation whatever with our religious beliefs. — the expression is a very common one but the same Chinese are the first to be puzzled when asked for the meaning. It is a personification of the providence, luck, justice, and also weather, and is as undefined a word as many others in Chinese. 雪花兒 hsüé³ hua¹ 'r, lit. snow-flowers, snow-flakes. 閙着頑兒 nao⁴ cho² uan² 'r, to play with, to make sport with.

TRANSLATION.

As soon I have gone out — the weather has become cloudy — folding my arms on my breast — I enter a tea-shop — I lean against the brick stove — and look for a friend from whom I may beg some money — as I go out of the tea-shop — here snow-flakes are falling — the old gentleman in the sky — only likes to make sport with us poor people.

XXIII

褡兒搭
褡連兒作親家
我和褡連兒親梳頭
親家的姑娘會梳子熟
一梳梳了個麪子
麥子磨成麪油
芝蔴磨成架
黃瓜上了架
茄子打提溜

NOTES

The beginning of the song does not seem to have any comprehensible meaning and I can only translate it literally. 褡連兒 ta¹ lien² 'r, cloth purse in which the chinese keep their banknotes, called also 錢褡連兒 ch'ien² ta¹ lien¹ 'r, money purse. Another sort is styled 檳榔褡連兒 ping¹ lang² ta¹ lien² 'r, and is used for holding betel nuts, as the name shows. 作親家 tsuo⁴ ch'in¹ chia¹, to become a relative. The word ch'in¹ chia¹ means all relations who bear a different family name. The word is in modern Pekinese wrongly pronounced ch'ing⁴ chia¹. 梳了個麥子熟 shu¹ la¹ ko⁴ mai⁴ tzŭ shou², she has taken as much time to comb her hair, as would be required for the wheat to become ripe in the fields. 上了架 "has grown on the bower". Cucumber plants are made creep on small bowers. 打提溜 ta³ ti¹ liu¹, to swing, pushed by the wind.

TRANSLATION

The purse, the purse — I have become a relation of the purse — the purse family's girl knows how to dress her hair — and has taken as much time to comb it as is required for the wheat to get ripe — for the wheat to be ground and made into flour — for the sesamum to be ground and made into ail — for the cucumber to grow on the bowers — and for the brinjal fruit to be swung by the wind.

XXXIV

羅鍋子橋
一磴兒到比一磴兒高
燈籠兒閙草水皮兒漂
金魚兒咬着銀魚尾兒
大肚子的蝦蟆
哇兒呱哇兒呱的叫

NOTES

This stanza is composed in praise of the fine scenery in the Emperor's Summer palace grounds, where the hunchbacked bridge is also to be seen. 一磴兒 i[1] teng[4] 'r, a step in a staircase, in a flight of stairs. 閙草 cha[2] ts'ao[3], grass wich grows near the gatelocks, called also 燈籠兒草 teng[1] lung[2] 'r ts'ao[3], "lantern grass" from its leaves being strung to a stalk like so many chinese lanterns to a rope. 金魚兒 chin[1] yü[2] 'r, "goldfish". 水皮兒 shuei[3] p'i[2] 'r, the surface of the water, lit. "the water skin". 銀魚兒 yin[2] yü[2] 'r, "silverfish".

TRANSLATION

On the hunchback bridge — one step is higher than the other — under the bridge the leaves of the lantern grass float on the water — the goldfish run after the silverfish and bite their tails — and the toads with big bellies — cry kurkuà kurkuà.

XXXV

東 嶽 廟
東 廊 下
東 廊 下 有 個 墪 兒
蹲 着 個 金 眼 綠 毛 龜 兒
解 南 來 了 個 鬼 兒
挑 着 一 担 水 兒
擱 下 水 兒 撿 根 棍 兒
單 打 金 眼 綠 毛 龜 兒 的 腿 兒

NOTES

東嶽 tung¹ yü⁴, one of the five sacred mountains, the 泰山 t'ai⁴ shan¹, in the Shantung province. 墪兒 tun¹ 'r, a small earth moud. Each verse ends with the character 兒 eur², which gives fun to the song.

TRANSLATION

In the temple of mount T'ai-shan — under the east verandah — under the east verandah there is an earth mound — on which squats a turtle with golden eyes and a shell covered with green moss — from the south has come a devil — bearing on his shoulders a load of water — he lays down the water, picks up a stick — and only strikes the legs of the turtle with golden eyes and the shell covered with moss.

XXXVI

大 娘 子 喝 酒
二 娘 子 筛
三 娘 子 棒 過 小 菜 碟 兒 來
四 娘 子 來 回 的 去 端 菜
五 娘 子 一 傍 把 座 兒 安 排
他 說 是 大 家 湊 個 團 圓 會
滑 拳 行 令 樂 開 懷

NOTES

大娘子 ta⁴ niang² tzŭ, is the wife of the first brother in the family. 二娘子 eur⁴ niang² tzŭ, is the wife of the second brother and so forth. 筛酒 shai¹ chiou³, to warm the wine before drinking it. 棒 p'eng³, to keep on one's hands, to present, to offer. 小菜兒 hsiao³ ts'ai⁴ 'r, salted vegetables with which the Chinese relish their food. 端菜 tuan¹ ts'ai⁴, to bring the food on the table. — 傍 i p'ang², by the side, aside. 團圓會 t'uan² yüan² huei⁴, general feast in which all the members of the family collect to dine together. This day falls on the fifteenth of the eighth month, because in that night the moon is perfectly-full 團圓 t'uan² yüan². 樺拳 hua² ch'iüan², to play at guessfingers, at morra. 行令 hsing² ling¹, literary amusement. Somebody in the company begins by giving a verse or a classical phrase, and the other members of society must follow by inventing another verse or phrase with the same rhyme, or with the same parallelism of words, or the same style of allusions. The man who first exhausts his tock of phrases is punished by being forced to drink a number of glasses of wine.

TRANSLATION

The first lady drinks w'ne — the second lady warms the wine — the third ladies come bringing in small saucers with salted cucumbers — the fourth lady at the side arranges the places (covers) — she says that every body has come for a complete meeting — to play at guessfingers, to play at allusions game, and to be merry.

XXXVII

禿子禿　　箍出油來
上腦箍　　煎豆腐

NOTES

These words are sung to tease the boys. who

have their hair shaven. 箍 ku¹, a whoop, an iron belt put about barrels. 腦箍 nao³ ku¹, is the name of an old instrument of torture consisting of a red hot circle of iron which was put on the head.

TRANSLATION

You baldhead — we will hut a red hot whoop round your head — and with the oil we will press out of it — we will fry bean-cake.

XXXVIII

搭兒連蓓
家親兒連蓓我
沉兒作姑和親
診病娘家家
壽藥把夫的請
膽把兒方個了
　　子蚊藥了開
　　心蚤是的開
斤半要兒髈翅蠅蒼虼

NOTES

The beginnig of this song is identical with that of song Nº 33. 診脈 chen⁴ muo⁴, to feel the pulse as chinese doctors do. 藥方 iao⁴ fang medical prescription written and signed by the physician.

蚊子 uen² tzu, the mosquito.　　蛞蚤 ko⁴ tsao³, the flea.
蒼蠅 ts'ang¹ ying², the fly.

TRANSLATION

The purse, the purse — I am now a relation of the purse family — but their daughter has grown dangerously sick — and they have called a physician who has felt her pulse — and then has written a prescription, and people have gone to buy the medicines — on the prescription there is written: mosquito's livers, flea's hearts and half a pound of flies wings.

XXXIX

三兒三兒
穿的是甚撒兒
穿的是青洋縐褲子
青洋縐汗襧兒
梳着個牛糞狐兒
左邊戴着晚香玉
右邊戴着茉莉花兒
五分底兒的雙臉兒鞋
漂白的襪子明期臉兒

NOTES

These words are addressed to a young girl, as

may be seen from the description of her dress, which follows. The slang word sa² 'r, not generally known even among Pekinese, means dress, fashion, toilette. As no written character exists to represent this sound and this meaning, I have used for it the character sa 撒 which being originally in the first tone, here ought to be read in the second. Wanting to find a character for the word, it could be formed this combination 㜢 to be read sa² 'r. — One of the phrases commonly heard is this 你有撒兒沒撒兒 ni³ iou³ sa² 'r, mei² sa² 'r ? — meaning "have you got a good dress or not? 洋縐 yang² chou⁴, crape imported by foreigners. 汗褟兒 han⁴ t'a¹ 'r, sort of cloth under-dress or shirt worn by Chinese in contact with the skin. European shirts are mostly styled 汗衫 han⁴ shan¹. 牛糞 niu² fen⁴ "ox-dung", name for a sort of head dress, more decently called 圓頭 yüan² t'ou² "round head". 㼷 p'ai³, character not noted in the dictionaries but mentioned by Sir T. Wade in his Tone exercises. It means "to let onself down, to lie down, and then to be seated, placed". Here it is used as a noun, and is referred to the chignon placed on the girl's head. 晚香玉 uan³ hsiang¹ yü⁴, the gem which smells in the evening, the tuberosa (lat. *Polianthes tuberosa*). 五分底兒 u³-fen¹ ti³ 'r, thick five fen. The fen is the tenth part of the ts'un, an inch. The shoe sole is called 底兒 ti³ 'r, or 底子 ti³ tzu. and may be as thick as five or six inches. That sort of heel which is placed sometimes in the center of the sole in ladies shoes is called 花盆底兒 hua¹ p'en² ti³ 'r, "flower-pot heel". 雙臉兒鞋 shuang¹ lien 'r hsie², literally "two faced shoes,, are so called when two ornamental leather strings, come from under the sole on the point of the shoe. 漂白 p'iao¹ pai², whitewashed, painted in white — the character 漂 is here vulgarly p'iao³. 明期臉兒 ming² ch'i lien³ 'r, chinese socks are so called when the seam is to be seen in the middle.

TRANSLATION

San'r, San'r, what sort of dress have you put on? — "I have put on trowsers made of foreign crape — and a shirt made of foreign crape — my hair is combed in a round chignon — on the left of it I have stuck a tuberose — and to the right a jasmine — then I have got shoes with a sole half-inch thick and with leather ornaments — and white socks with the seam to be seen outside.

XL

咩咩羊　　　　抓把草
跳花牆　　　　餵他娘

NOTES

咩 mie¹, the sheep's bleating. 他娘 t'a¹ niang², the small sheep's mother. This is one of those little songs the mothers teach their children, when they begin to speak.

TRANSLATION

The bleating small sheep — has jumped over the flowery wall — to catch a bunch of grass — and to feed her mother.

XLI

大 翻 車
小 翻 車
一 翻 翻 了 個 花 大 姐
紅 裙 兒
綠 襖 兒
丁 香 小 脚 兒
對 面 喝 酒 兒
倒 像 親 姐 兒 倆

NOTES

The beginning of this song is not clear; it appears that the disposition of words in the first and in the second verse is irregular, saying 大翻車 小翻車 ta⁴ fan¹ tch'o¹-hsiao³ fan ch'o instead of 大車翻 小車翻 ta⁴ ch'o¹ fan¹-hsiao³ ch'o¹ fan¹, meaning the big cart has overturned, the small cart has overturned. Furthermore the song speaks at the beginning of only one girl and it ends with two. That shows the song is not complete and every cart is supposed to be occupied by a girl. 花大姐 hua¹ ta⁴ chie³, lit. "a flowery elder sister" means, a beautiful and well dressed girl. It is also said in the same sense 花妞兒 hua¹ niu¹ 'r. 丁香 ting hsiang, clove, very small feet are compared to grains of clove.

TRANSLATION

A big cart has overturned — a small cart has overturned — and a very beautiful young lady has fallen out of one — (and another young lady has fallen too) — with a red petticoat — and a green overcoat — with feet as small as grains of clove — they drink wine one in front of the other — and really are very much like two sisters.

XLII

高高山上一座小廟兒
裏頭坐着個神道兒
頭上戴頂羅帽兒
身上穿件外套兒
兩個小鬼喝道兒
四個小鬼抬着籐轎兒
出了門兒一遭兒
出巡回來歸廟兒

NOTES

神道 shen² tao⁴, a spirit. 外套兒 uai⁴ t'ao⁴ 'r, "external cover" is a sort of long dress, worn externally. 喝道兒 ho¹ tao⁴ 'r, and also 喝道子 ho¹ tao⁴ tzŭ, to shout before the chair of an official to make way. 籐轎 t'eng² chiao⁴, a light chair made of rattan. 一遶兒 i jao⁴ 'r, a turn, a stroll. 出巡 ch'u¹ hsün¹, to go out on a tour of inspection.

TRANSLATION

On a very high mountain there is a small temple — and inside sits a spirit — he wears on his head a crape-hat — and wears on his body a long gown — two small devils go in front shouting for room — four small devils bear the rattan-chair — he has gone out for a stroll — to make an inspection and then returning comes back to the temple.

XLIII

新打一把茶壺亮堂堂
新買一個小豬兒不吃糠
新娶一個媳婦兒不吃飯
眼淚汪汪想他親娘

NOTES

打 ta³, to beat, to strike, to work in metal. 亮

堂堂 liang⁴ t'ang¹ t'ang¹, very bright; the character 堂 is originally read in the second tone, but here is pronounced in the first. 糠 k'ang¹, husks of grain with which pigs are fed.

TRANSLATION

A newly made metal tea-kettle is very bright — a newly bought small pig does not eat husks of grain — a newly married wife does not take food — she weeps profusely and thinks of her mother.

XLIV

冲 冲 喜 兒 門 進 一
棚 大 搭 頭 裏 子 院
點 燈 把 子 屋 房 洞
盈 盈 淚 傍 一 娘 姑 新
觀 回 來 的 住 不 郎 新
兒 西 東 兒 點 吃 不 你 說
疼 心 可 我

NOTES

This song contains a sketch of marriage ceremonies. 喜冲冲 hsi³ ch'ung¹ ch'ung¹ very merrily and with much noise. The character 冲 ch'ung means to shake, to dash against, but here it is only used to mean confusion, hurry, disorder. 洞房 tung⁴ fang², the bridal room. 淚盈盈 lei⁴ ying¹ ying, with many tears. 盈盈 ying¹ ying, flowing, in great quantity, said of tears. The character 盈 is here in the first tone, but its regular tone is the second, and ought to be read ying². 新郎 hsin¹ lang², the bridegroom. 不住的 pu⁴ chu⁴ ti, without interruption. 來回 lai² huei², repeatedly.

TRANSLATION

Entering the gate, how merry it is! — in the courtyard they have raised a big shed — in the bridal room the lamp is lighted — the bride in a corner is weeping bitterly — the bridegroom repeatedly calls to her — and says: if you do not take some food — my heart will ache.

XLV

和尚和尚搖鈴鐺
嘚兒嗒嗖喝我騎上
騎到那兒去
騎到天邊兒去

NOTES

This song is repeated by boys to ridicule the buddhist priests who go round begging, and read their sacred books shaking a small bell. They are therefore compared to asses and mules which are similarly provided with bells. 鈴鐺 ling² tang¹, a small bell — 旦兒搭 pronounce törtà, a peculiar voice to get the mule, or the ass to walk. - There are of course no characters for it and those written above not only are completely arbitrary, but do not exactly correspond to the pronunciation. The same is to be said for the word 倭喝 uo-ho, which has the same meaning.

TRANSLATION

Oh the bonze, the bonze is shaking the bell — go ahead! I will ride him — ride how far? — as far as the boundary of the sky.

XLVI

小回回兒
怎麼那麼奸
四兩猪肉約半天
左嫌小右嫌少
抱着猪頭往家跑

NOTES

These words are sung to insult Mohammedans who are not allowed to eat pork. 左右 tsuo³ iuo⁴, right and left (the Chinese right hand being the European left hand). Means now and now, several times, repeatedly.

TRANSLATION

The small Mohammedan — how deceitful is he! — to buy only four ounces of pork, he is weighing for a good half-day — now he complains it is little and then he complains again it is little — then folding in his arms a pig's head he runs home.

XLVII

一呀二呀三棍兒
倒打連棍兒五
花打兒銅錢數
銅錢鏨鏨兒六
鏨鏨銀錠兒七
銀錠花花打打兩丈一
花花兩甚麼兩
兩馬掌
二甚麼二兒
雙夾棍兒
雙甚麼雙
虎槓槍
虎甚麼虎
牛皮鼓
牛甚麼牛

磕郎毡
磕甚麼磕
燕子窩
燕甚麼燕
扯花線
扯甚麼扯
孫臏扯
孫甚麼孫
呂洞賓
呂甚麼呂
李楊兒癩
癩甚麼癩
竈王爺
竈甚麼竈
城隍廟
城甚麼城

肚兒疼
肚甚麽肚
搖葫蘆
搖甚麽搖

雪花兒飄
雪甚麽雪‧
孫猴兒倒打猪八戒

NOTES

Chinese children practice a game which is also known by boys in foreign countries. Two boys sit one facing the other and strike first their own hands together and then each other's. To keep measure with the movement they mark, the time with these words, which are meaningless, and are huddled together only for the sake of the final rhymes. The game is called 打花巴掌 ta³ hua¹ pa¹ chang³. 呀 ya¹, is purely phonetic and meaningless. 倒打 tao⁴ ta³, to strike alternately — here the character 倒 is pronounced in the fourth and not in the third tone. 連三棍兒 lien² san¹ kun⁴ 'r, uninterruptedly three sticks (that is to say three blows). 數 in the third tone shu³, means to calculate, to reckon. 鏨 tsan, to carve, to chisel. 鏨子 tsan⁴ tzŭ, a chisel. 銀錠 yin² ting⁴, an ingot of silver. 夾棍兒 chia¹ kun⁴ 'r, an instrument of torture to squeeze the ankles lit. squeezing sticks. 嗑郎毬 k'o¹ lang¹ ch'iu²; I cannot find any explanation of this. The Chinese say that they do not know the meaning of the word. All that I could get from them is that the vulgar word k'o¹-lang 'r, means a corner, and is used instead of the more common 噶拉兒 ka¹-la² 'r (written according to Sir Thomas Wade's manner). The word ch'iu² is a ball. Could it be an "empty ball"? 孫臏 Sun¹-pin¹ a remarkable minister in the old state of Jen; generally known by all children. 呂洞賓 Lü³ tung⁴ pin¹, one of the eight genii. 鐵柺李 t'ie³ kuai³ li³, another of the eight genii, a lame man called also: 瘸柺李 ch'üe² kuai³ li³, 竈王爺 tsao⁴ uang² ye², The god of the cooking stoves, familiar chinese god to whom a sacrifice is offered the 23ᵈ day of the twelfth moon. The god is said to have a wife called 竈王奶奶 tsao⁴ uang² nai² nai³; she is worshipped in chinese families, but not in the shops, in which only the Tsao-uang is worshipped. 城隍廟 ch'eng² huang² miao⁴, the tutelar god of chinese cities. 搖葫蘆 iao² hu² lu², to shake a pumpkin, one of the favourite amusements of chinese babies, who are very often seen deeply absorbed in shaking a small calabash. 孫猴兒 sun¹ hou²'r, the monkey traveller in the novel 西遊記 Hsi¹-yu²-chi⁴, Recollections of wanderings in the west countries. 猪八戒 chu¹ pa¹ chie⁴, a pig spoken of in the same novel as lazy and uxorious and therefore severely beaten by the monkey who was in charge of his education. These notions although taken from a novel in literary style, yet are generally known by the people, that have besides many ditties and rhymes on the subject.

TRANSLATION

One, two — let us strike alternately three

blows — five flowery sticks — count the cash — six chisels — seven ingots of silver — let us strike as long as two chang and one foot (!) — two, what two? — two horse shoes — two, what two? — a pair of squeezing sticks — a pair, what pair? — the tiger bears a gun on its shoulders — tiger, what tiger? — a drum covered with ox skin — ox, what ox? — an empty ball (?) — K'o⁴, what K'o⁴? — a swallow's nest — swallow, what swallow? — pull the flowery thread — pull, what pull? — Sun pin pulls — Sun, what Sun? — Lü³-tung⁴ pin — Lü³, what Lü³? — The lame genius Ch'üe² kuai³ 'r li³ — Ch'üe², what ch'üe? — The god of the cooking stoves. — Stove, what stove? — The god protector of the city — City, what city? — The belly aches — belly, what belly? — shake the pumpkin — shake, what shake? — Snow-flakes are whirling round — snow, what snow? — The monkey Sun¹ Chu¹-po¹-chie⁴,

---

XLVIII

正月正
正月裏個蓮花兒燈
打花巴掌的
老太太愛逛個蓮花兒
燒着香兒念着佛兒
茉莉茉莉花兒串枝蓮
打花巴掌的二月二
老太太愛吃個白糖棍兒
燒着香兒念着佛兒

蓮烟蓮

枝三東兒枝四刺兒

串月關佛串月摘佛

兒三個着兒四不着兒

花的吃念花的魚

莉掌愛兒莉掌吃

莉巴太香茉巴太香

茉花太着莉花太着

茉打老燒茉打老燒

蓮薯蓮肉蓮鷄蓮鴨蓮

枝五白兒枝六煮兒枝七煮兒枝八燉兒枝九

串月白佛串月白佛串月白佛串月白佛串月

兒五個着兒六個着兒七個着兒八個着兒九

花的吃念花的吃念花的吃念花的吃念花的

莉掌愛兒莉掌愛兒莉掌愛兒莉掌愛兒莉掌

莉巴太香茉巴太香茉巴太香茉巴太香茉巴

茉花太着莉花太着莉花太着莉花太着莉花

茉打老燒茉打老燒茉打老燒茉打老燒茉打

老太太愛吃個白花藕
燒着香兒念着佛兒
茉莉茉莉花兒串枝蓮
打花巴掌的十月一
老太太愛吃個雪花梨
燒着香兒念着佛兒
茉莉茉莉花兒串枝蓮

NOTES

This song, like the last one is also sung by boys when playing at 打花巴掌 ta³ hua¹ pa¹ chang³. 正月正 cheng¹ yüo⁴ cheng¹, the first moon. 蓮花燈 lien² hua¹ teng¹, Lantern made of paper and shaped like a lotus flower. 逛燈 kuang⁴ teng¹, means to go out on the streets to look at the different shows of lanterns exhibited during five days, from the thirteenth to the seventeenth in the first month in the year. The regular day for the show is the 15th on which falls the 燈節 teng¹ chie² feast of lanterns. 念着佛 nien⁴ cho Fuo³, uttering prayers before Buddha. 串枝蓮 ch'uan⁴ chih¹ lien², a wild flower not unlike the lotus. This refrain is repeated at every couplet. We translate it only once. 白糖棍兒 pai² t'ang² kun¹'r, small sugar sticks bought by children. 關東烟 kuan¹ tung¹ yen¹, tobacco from Manchuria, the best quality of tobacco. 摘刺 chai² tz'u⁴, to take away the bones from a fish. 生白薯 sheng¹ pai² shu³, uncooked sweet potato. 燉鴨 tun¹ ya¹, a stewed duck. 白花藕 pai² hua¹ ou³, a flour made from the root-stock of the lotus. 雪花梨 hsüe³ hua¹ li², sort of very good pears found in Shantung, whose pulp is said to be as white as flakes of snow.

TRANSLATION

Strike the hands, in the first month of the year — the old lady likes to go out to look at the lotus-lanterns — burning incense and saying prayers — with jasmines, jasmines and wild lotus — Strike the hands, the second day of the second moon — the old lady likes to eat sugar sticks — Strike the hands, the third day of the third moon — the old lady likes to smoke Manchurian tobacco. Strike the hands, the fourth day of the fourth moon — the old lady likes to eat fish without taking the bones away. — Strike the hands, the fifth of the fifth moon — the old lady likes to eat raw yams — strike the hands, the sixth day of the sixth moon — the old lady likes to eat boiled pork — strike the hands, the seventh day of the seventh moon — the old lady likes to eat a boiled chicken with no sauce — strike the hands, the eighth day of the eighth moon — the old lady likes to eat stewed duck — strike the hands, the ninth day of the ninth moon — the old lady likes to eat lotus root flour — strike the hand, the first day of the tenth moon — the old lady likes to eat snow-white pears.

XLIX

打 羅 兒 篩
曳 羅 兒 篩
麥 子 熟 了 請 你 的 伯
你 伯 愛 吃 肉 兒 的
你 叔 愛 吃 豆 兒 的

NOTES

These words are not heard within the walls of Peking, but in the country. 羅兒 luo²'r a sift to bolt flour. 曳 ye⁴, to drag, to pull, to shake. 伯 read by the peasants not puo² but pai¹, one's father's elder brother. This character is read also pai³, in the word 大伯子 ta⁴ pai³ tzu, title given to a man by his younger brother's wife. 叔 shu² read here shou², as the peasants do. One's father's younger brother.

TRANSLATION

Beating the sieve sift! — shaking the sieve sift! — when the wheat is ripe, we will invite your uncle — your elder uncle likes to eat meat — your younger uncle likes to eat beans.

L

一副筐兒繩扁擔遊九城
八根兒挑起了
賣蔥阿兒
賣蒜阿兒
賣青菜兒
打鼓兒
喝雜銀錢兒
唉首飾來賣

NOTES

These words are sung by children to imitate the perambulating vendors in the street. 一副筐 i¹ fu⁴ k'uang¹ a pair of baskets hanging from the pole called 扁擔 pien³ tan. 八根兒繩 pa¹ ken¹'r sheng², eight strings. As every basket is attached to an end of the pole by four strings, so eight strings comes to mean a porter's pole and more generally every sort of small chinese industry practiced by vendors furnished with such a pole. 九城 chiu³ ch'eng², the nine cities, the city of Peking. 青菜 ch'ing¹ ts'ai⁴ every sort of green vegetable. After speaking of the vendors of vegetables the song comes to speak of a curious sort of small industry practiced in Peking. Two men go together. One marches forward and beats a little drum, the other bearing on the shoulder a pole with baskets calls loudly for people who are willing to sell silver head-ornaments, or other small objects of value. This proceeding is called 喝雜銀錢 ho¹ tsa² yin² ch'ien², to call for different (and bad quality) silver to buy them for ready money.

TRANSLATION

With a pair of baskets — are provided all the small pedlars — with pole and baskets they go all over the city — to sell onions — to sell garlic — to sell green vegetables — the man who beats the drum — and the other who cries: I buy objects of silver — ohè, (who has got) head ornaments let him come and sell.

LI

翻餅烙餅
油炸餡兒餅
翻過來瞧瞧

NOTES

Chinese boys playing together take each other by the hands and then turn round without separating the hands. The movement of turning round is likened to the action of turning a pie on the pan, and so this game is called 翻餅烙餅 fan¹ ping³ lao⁴ ping³. 烙餅 lao⁴ ping³, to cook a pie. 油炸 iu²-cha², fried in the oil.

TRANSLATION

Turn the pie, cook the pie — the pie with stuffing fried in oil — turn it round and let us sel.

LII

高高山上一落磚兒
磚兒上坐着個老太太兒
三根頭髮馬尾纂兒
一心要戴個凉凉簪兒

NOTES

一落磚兒 i¹ luo⁴ chuan¹'r, a pile of bricks 馬尾纂兒 ma³ i³ tsuan³ 'r, sort of sham chignon made of the hair of a horse tail. — 心 i¹ hsin¹, she has no other thought but, compare latin *"toto corde"*. 凉凉簪兒 summer hair-pins; during the summer ladies are supposed to lay aside silver-pins and to wear jade pins and also jade bracelets and rings. People who cannot afford to buy jade pins, get for a trifling sum pins made of glass, imitating the jade. These last are called **liang² liang² tsan¹'r**.

TRANSLATION.

On a very high mountain there is a pile of bricks. — On the bricks there is sitting an old lady — with three hairs and a false horse-tail chignon — and she only thinks that she wants to wear summer pins on her hair.

LIII

鞋兒窖兒底兒厚幫
我到娘家一坐熱
哥哥說炕上坐
嫂子說炕不熱
哥哥說搬板凳
嫂子說搬不動
哥哥說搬椅子
嫂子說沒腿子
哥哥說給妹妹點兒錢
嫂子說還半年
哥哥說給妹妹點兒米
嫂子說還不起
我也不吃你們的飯
我也不喝你們的酒
瞧瞧親娘我就走

出門兒遇見個大黃狗
撕了我的裙兒
咬了我的手
忍心的哥哥出來打打狗

NOTES

Chinese wives are allowed from time to time to visit their old family, and to stay there for some days. Here this song depicts the grief of a wife who goes to visit her mother, arrived there she meets with her brother who treats her well and with her sister-in-law who hates her. The words are simple and touching. 厚底兒鞋 hou⁴ ti³ 'r hsie², shoes with a thick heel. 幫兒窄 pang¹ eur chai³, the heel-band is narrow, and therefore it is painful to walk. Pang¹ eur is "the leather heel-band of a shoe, for strengthening the back of a shoe" (Giles). 娘家 niang² chia¹, a wife's family. 走一百 tsou³ i⁴ pai³ I walk a hundred, it is understood 里地 li³ ti⁴, chinese miles. The k'ang⁴, chinese brick bed is warmed during winter by fuel. 板凳 pan³ teng⁴, a wooden stool. 還半年 huan² pan⁴ nien², it may be understood so " to give her a little money we shall borrow it and then we shall not be able to repay it back until after a good half-year". 還不起 huan² pu⁴ ch'i³, in the same meaning, we shall not be able to give it back to the person who lends the rice to us. The expression pu⁴ ch'i³ following the verb, that verb acquires a negative potential meaning, as not to be able to... or better corresponding to the Chinese, " not to be up to..." 忍心 jen³ hsin¹, these words are a reproach to the brother, meaning you who may tolerate in your heart that I suffer so much, meaning that the brother after all his good intentions lets his wife do as she likes.

TRANSLATION

With high-heeled shoes — and narrow heel-bands — I walk a hundred *li* to arrive at my home, — My elder brother says: Sit on the k'ang⁴ — my sister-in-law says: the k'ang is not warm — my elder brother says: bring here a wooden stool — my sister-in-law says: it cannot be brought round — my elder brother says: bring here a chair — my sister-in-law says: the chair has no legs — my elder brother says: give your younger sister some money — the sister-in-law says: we would take half a year to pay it back — my elder brother says: give your gounger sister a little rice — the sister-in-law says, we could not give it back to the lender — But I will not eat your rice — and I will not drink your wine — I will only see my mother and then go away — going out of the gate I have met with a big yellow dog — that has torn my apron — and has bitten my hand — My patient elder brother, come out and beat the dog!

LIV

杜棃兒花了剪會哭哭過丈母家小豆粥不死你的禿了頭
開白活起搭也也婿母還
養
拿
嘎
爹
娘
女
丈
我
碾
熬
餓

樹頭子了瞎給人作甚麼搭家
母哭穀丈別斗勸你二來母有兒

NOTES

These words are sung to small girls by their parents. The first two verses have nothing to do with the rest, but, as a girl is the subject of the song, they fit very well. 杜棃兒 tu⁴ li⁴ 'r, a pear with small fruit *(Pyrus betulaefolia)*. 瞎嘎搭 hsia¹ ka² ta¹, familiar expression, it means to make noise using a pair of scissors and without good effect, and it is said of the small girls who begin to learn how to cut the cloth to make dresses of it. Hsia¹ originally means blind, and then irregularly, badly as a blind man could do. 給人家 kei³ jen² chia¹, they give (the parents) her to people, that is to say they get her married. 豆兒粥 tou⁴ 'r chou, a gruel made of rice and beans. 禿丫頭 t'u¹ ya¹ t'ou² bald-headed servant, title given in the family to small girls, who are generally called by their parents ya¹ huan² or 丫頭 ya¹ t'ou². 餓不死 ngo⁴ pu⁴ ssu³, negative potential form, she cannot be starved to death.

TRANSLATION

The small pear-tree — has opened its white flowers — to bring to light a small girl — what is the use of it? — she begins first to take the scissors and to cut badly the cloth — then when she has learned to cut the cloth, one must give her up to other people — the father also weeps — the mother also weeps — the bridegroom comes over to console his mother-in-law — and says: mother-in-law, mother-in-law, do not weep — I have got at home three pecks of grain — we will grind the oats — and boil a rice congee with beans — so that your bald-headed daughter shall not be starved to death.

LV

紅葫蘆
軋腰兒
我是爺爺的肉姣兒

我是哥哥的親妹子
我是嫂子的氣包兒
爺爺賠甚麼
爺爺賠姑娘
爺爺賠甚麼
大奶奶賠姑娘
大奶奶賠甚麼
大奶奶賠姑娘
大奶奶賠甚麼
針線笸籮兒賠姑娘
哥哥賠甚麼
哥哥賠姑娘
哥哥賠甚麼
花布手巾賠姑娘
嫂嫂嫂嫂賠甚麼
破爛鞾子氊子
打發那丫頭嫁漢子

NOTES

The words are supposed to be said by a small girl. 紅葫蘆 hung² hu² lu², red pumpkin; the boys who have not enough money to buy playthings, content themselves with pumpkins which they go whirling about. 軋腰兒 ya⁴ yao¹ 'r, "with crushed sides" is the name of a sort of pumpkin shaped in the form of two balls placed one on the other. Cutting this pumpkin in the middle one has two cups. As to the relation between these words to what follows, I suppose the girl speaks of herself as of a precious little thing, because that kind of pumpkin is sometimes appreciated by the Chinese who buy the smallest for two or three taels, and wear them on the body as an ornament. 肉姣兒

jou⁴ chiao¹ 'r, lit. "my flesh dear", an endearing term for a little girl, meaning to say: you are my own flesh and blood. 氣包兒 ch'i⁴ pao¹ 'r, curious expression said of a person who has the privilege of irritating somebody constantly. The literal translation would be "the wrath-bundle". The small girl speaks so because it is generally admitted and practiced in chinese families that the elder brother's wife carries on continual warfare with her sisters-in-law. Afterwards the girl pretends to want to know what their relations will give her on her wedding day. To give cadeaux to a bride to form her dowry is called 賠 p'ei², or more completely 賠送 p'ei² sung⁴. 奶奶 nai³ nai,³ one's father's mother. The bannermen call nai³ nai³ a mother. 針線笸籮 chen¹ hsien⁴ p'uo³ luo², a basket where needles, pin, thread, scissors are kept and everything else required for ladies' work. 姑娘 ku¹-niang², is here used instead of the personal pronoun thou or you. 罈子 t'an¹ tzŭ, a big bottle to contain salt vegetables, water and also coal. 鑵子 kuan⁴-tzŭ, other sort of vessel made of porcelain or of earthenware. 嫁漢子 chia⁴ han⁴ tzŭ to marry a husband, a man. Here it would perhaps be better to translate "a fellow" as the woman's words are not inspired with friendly feelings altogether.

TRANSLATION

The red pumpkin — has crushed sides — I am my grandfather's "own dear flesh and blood" —

I am my brother's "carnal sister" — and I am my sister-in-law's "bundle of wrath" — grandfather, grandfather, what will you give me at my marriage? — "I will give you a big chest and a big wardrobe" — "Grandmother, grandmother, what will you give me?" — "I will give you a work basket" — "Elder brother, elder brother, what will you give me?" — "I will give you a fancy cloth towel" — Sister-in-law, sister-in-law, what will you give me?" — "A broken jar — and a smashed bottle — and send you, that girl, away to marry a fellow".

LVI

樹葉兒黑
呀呀喲子煤
小黑兒長的像李逵
呲着牙兒瞪着眼兒
手裏揩着個黑鞭杆兒
騎着黑牛兒
喫着個黑麵餅兒
一上上在山頂兒

NOTES

These words are sung to children of a brown complexion. The second verse is simply a refrain with no meaning. 小黑兒 hsiao³ hei¹ 'r, nickname given to a brown child. The word hei¹ contains all the shades of colour from black to brown. 李逵 Li³ k'uei², a celebrated brigand in the Sung dynasty, who was of a brown complexion. He is spoken of in the Novel 水滸 shuei³ hu³. His nickname was 黑旋風 hei¹hsüan² feng¹, the black whirlwind. 呰着牙 tzǔ¹ cho¹ ya², showing the teeth.

TRANSLATION

The tree-leaves are dark — yaya yüetzu mei — the small brown boy is very like Li-k'uei — showing his teeth and staring — he grasps in his hand a black whip-stick — he rides on a black ox — eats a cake made of black flour — and going up he gets as far as the mountain summit.

LVII

荊條棍兒
用處兒多
編了柳斗兒
編笸籮
笸籮倒比柳斗兒大
管着柳斗兒叫哥哥

NOTES

荊 ching¹ is instead of 荊蒿花 ching¹ hao¹ hua¹, the *Vitex incisa*, with stems of which baskets are woven. 柳斗 liou³ tou³, a measure made of willow branches; sometimes it is made of *Vitex* stems, but it is even then called a "willow-peck". 管着 kuan³-cho¹, with regard to, giving a denomination. 荊條棍兒 ching¹ t'iao² kun⁴ 'r stems of *Vitex*.

TRANSLATION

The stems of the *Vitex incisa* — are fit for many uses — one may make of it a "willow-peck" — and one may make of it a basket — the basket is indeed larger than the willow-peck — and calls the willow peck "elder brother".

LVIII

鐵籩豆
大把兒抓
娶了個媳婦兒就不要媽
要媽就要叉
要叉就分家

NOTES

The first two verses with which the song begins are called 頭子 t'ou² tzŭ "head". They do not seem to have here any relation with the meaning of the following words. The song speaks about some cases in which new-married men forget the duty of obedience to their own mother, and want to set up a family by themselves. The words are ironical and there is in them a sense of reproach and grief. 鐵 t'ie³, iron, here "as hard as iron". 蠶豆 ts'an² tou⁴, broad beans, which are sold to children on the streets for the modest sum of a ta for a handful. 大把兒 ta⁴ pa³ 'r, a big handful. 耍叉 shua³ ch'a¹, to fight with a pronged stick, metaph. for "to quarrel". 分家 fen¹ chia¹, to set up an autonomous family, to separate from the old stock.

TRANSLATION.

Broad beans as hard as iron — to be had in big handfuls — after having married a wife, then he does not want his mother — if he wanted his mother then they would quarrel — and if they quarrelled, then he ought to separate from the old house.

LIX

娶媳婦兒的
門口兒過
十二個傍細樂
宮燈戳燈扇
旗鑼傘扇
八個鼓手奏
姑娘走
轎子抬着姑娘的大門口
抬到婆家的大門
進門兒入洞房

去會小新郎
娶了三年並二載
丫頭小子沒處兒擺

NOTES

娶媳婦兒的 ch'ü³ hsi² fu⁴ 'r ti, the persons who go to fetch the bride and take her to the bridegroom's house. A marriage procession. 宮燈 kung¹ teng¹, "palace lanterns" a sort of lanterns taken in hand by people in the marriage cortège. They are made with silk, or glass doors, and have no lighted candles in them. 戳燈 ch'uo¹ teng¹, another kind of lanterns fixed on a long stick, which may be stuck in the ground. 鼓手 ku³ shou³, literally "drum-hands" general name for all musicians who accompany the bride-chair. Some beat drums, other play on a sort of trumpet called 鎖吶 suo³ na¹. These men are also called 吹鼓手的 ch'ui¹ ku³ shou³ ti. 奏樂 tsou⁴ yüe⁴, to play solemn music. 細樂 hsi⁴ yüe⁴, a concert, a supposed harmony produced by different instruments. 婆家 p'uo² chia¹, mother-in-law, mother-in-law's family, in the husband's family. 小新郎 hsiao³ hsin¹ lang², the young bridegroom. 二載 two years. 三年並二載 san¹ nien² ping⁴ eur¹ tsai³, a curious expression to mean 5 years.

TRANSLATION

The bridal procession — passes by the gate —

there are twelve "palace lanterns" and "fixed lanterns" — banners, gongs, umbrellas, fans are on each side — eight musicians produce music — the chair which contains the girl passes on — and brings her as far as her mother-in-law's family house-gate — she enters the door and goes into the bridal room — she goes to stay with her young bridegroom — after having married her these five years there are so many babies and girls that there is no more room in the house for them.

LX

娘脆
要薄
不兒薄籬
長兒窩籬
巴婦吃兒
尾媳要閒錢
了媽有婦
雀了媽婦兒上
喜娶媽沒媳備
去買打媳婦兒媳婦兒你吃黎

NOTES

This song is inspired by the same feeling as song N° 58. 窩兒薄脆 uo¹ 'r pao² ts'uei⁴, sort of very hard and cheap cake. 笊籬 chao¹ li², a big spoon made of willow stems and used to take food out of the pan. The current phrase "we have no idle money to mend the willow spoon" means that a person has no intention of spending money for useless things, as would be to mend a willow spoon. 打皮 ta³ p'i², to peel a fruit.

TRANSLATION

The magpie has a long tail — after he has taken a wife he no more wants his mother — when his mother wants to eat some cheap cake — then (he says) "there is no idle money to mend willow spoons" — when his wife wants to eat pears — then he gets ready his ass — and goes to the market — when he has bought the pears — he peels them — and asks wife, wife, will you eat pears?

LXI

小禿兒
長檠兒
你媽養活一對雙棒兒
多大了
會走咧
你媽肚子裏又有了咧

NOTES

These words are addressed by one boy to another

in a joking way. 小禿兒 hsiao³ t'u¹ 'r, the small baldhead, the boy, used here instead of the personal pronoun "you". 長樣兒 chang³ yang⁴ 'r, he is grown up, lit. "his figure has grown". 養活 yang³ huo², to bear of women; it means also to nourish, to give food. 雙棒兒 shuang¹ pang¹ 'r, twins, in literary language they are called 雙生 shuang¹ sheng¹.

TRANSLATION

You small bald-heads — are grown up — your mother has born a couple of twins — how old are they? — "they can walk" — "your mother is again in the family way".

LXII

花紅柳綠線兒
又買針兒
又買線兒
又買王媽媽褲腿帶兒

NOTES

These words are for young girls who want to begin to work early with needle and thread. 花紅 hua¹ hung², as red as red flowers are. 柳綠 liou³ lü⁴, as green as willow-trees are 褲腿帶兒 k'u⁴ t'uei³ tai⁴ 'r, cloth bands used by women to bind the trowsers to their ankles.

TRANSLATION

I want red thread as red as red flowers and green thread as green as green willows — and I want to buy needles — and to buy more thread — and to buy ankle-bands for mother Wang.

LXIII

糊糊
糊 狗 肉 嘔
大 鍋 裏 香
二 鍋 裏 臭
請 王 媽 媽 來 吃 狗 肉 嘔

NOTES

Dog meat is a much appreciated dish in China. The character 糊 hu², is used here in want of another, and is pronounced hu¹, in the first tone. It means a special chinese way of preparing meat, by smearing it with sauce and then having it roasted in a pan. There is in the western city a restaurant called 狗肉居 kou³ jou⁴ chü¹, where roasted dog meat is provided for "amateurs". 嘔 ou⁴, phonetic character with no meaning here.

TRANSLATION

Roast, roast — roast dog meat, oh! — the first

pan smells — and the second pan stinks — I beg mother Wang to come and eat dog meat, oh!

LXIV

禿禿鎈
光光鎈
廟裏的和尙無頭髮
你撘磚兒
我撘瓦兒
單打和尙的禿光把兒

NOTES

Chinese boys do not show much reverence towards the priests, for whom they always have a ready collection of songs, epigrams and epithets. One of the general names with which Buddhist priests are gratified is 禿驢 t'u¹ lu², a bald ass. 鎈 ch'a¹, small cymbals used as toys; there is no character for the word and I used, in fault of better, this character; its original tone however is the first. As these cymbals are very bright and shining, the pates of bonzes are likened to them. 禿光把兒 t'u¹ kuang¹ pan³ 'r, a bald and shining pate.

TRANSLATION

Bald bald cymbals — shining, shining cymbals

the bonzes in the temple have no hair — you fling bricks and I fling tiles — only to strike the bonzes' bald pates.

LXV

煤 模 兒　　　杜 黎 子
炒 豆 兒　　　咕 咕 哝 兒

NOTES

Coal dust is mixed up with sand and water and then put into small wood square boxes, out of which the coal comes in the form of a small brick. This sort of coal is called 煤 齻 兒 mei² chien³ 'r. When pekinese boys are so lucky as to get hold of one of those wood-boxes called 煤 模 兒 mei² mu² 'r, they put inside of it all their small property, as toys, or food. 咕 咕 哝 兒, ku¹ ku¹ tiu¹ 'r, seeds of dates.

TRANSLATION

(In) the coal-mould — (there are) roast beans — small pears — and date seeds.

LXVI

丫 頭 丫
會 看 家

米蔴細蜜糕燒頭叫姥姥
老芝蔴爐兒火的了
偷換芝油棗熱撐

NOTES

油爐蜜 iu² cha² mi⁴, sort of sweet cake made of flower, sugar and honey, and then fried in oil. 棗兒糕 tsao³ 'r kao, pudding of date jam. 火燒 huo³ shao¹, "roasted on the fire" name of a cake. 撐的 ch'eng¹ ti, with a full stomach from having eaten too much.

TRANSLATION

The small girl — knows how to watch the house — she steals old rice — and barters it for sesamum seeds — the sesamum seeds are small — (and then) a sweet cake — a date-pudding — and a roasted cake — the small girl feels so overeaten that she calls for her grandmother.

LXVII

玲瓏塔
塔玲瓏

三層寶塔

十三層廟一座
廟內有老僧方丈
老僧方丈名頭青點僧
把奔磬笙管鐘說法念經
寶塔有老僧方丈名青頭愣僧點葫蘆會打棒吹撞會說會念
玲前有老僧當有六個叫愣僧點葫蘆會會會會會
玲塔廟內老徒弟一個個個個個叫叫是是奔奔把把頭頭頭頭點點點葫葫
玲塔廟老徒弟一個一個一個一個一個青愣僧點奔把

NOTES

玲瓏 ling² lung², elegant, pleasant, smart. 老僧 lao³ seng¹, an old buddhist priest. 方丈 fang¹ chang⁴, the abbot in a buddhist monastery. 徒弟 t'u² ti⁴, pupils who are supposed to learn the law and read the sacred books to become priests afterwards. 青頭愣 ch'ing¹ t'ou² leng⁴, expression impossible to translate; it is applied by Chinese in a despising sense to different objects, as for instance to an unripe fruit, or to a scorpion. 磬 ch'ing⁴ a musical stone used as a bell. 笙 sheng¹, a sort of pipe. 捧笙 p'eng³ sheng¹, to hold the sheng near the mouth by the two hands, that is to say, to play the sheng. 管 kuan³, a flute. 撞鐘 chuang⁴ chung¹, to strike the bell; chinese bells are not provided with a clapper, but are struck from outside by means of a wood truncheon hanging by cords at a small distance from the bell. 說法 shuo¹ fa⁴, to speak about the law, to recite a pious sermon.

TRANSLATION

How elegant is the pagoda! — how the pagoda is elegant! — the elegant pagoda has thirteen stores — before the pagoda there is a temple — in the temple there is an old bonze — the old bonze acts as abbot — and has by himself six pupils — one is called — Ch'ing¹ t'ou² leng⁴. — one is called Leng⁴ t'ou² ch'ing¹ — one is Seng¹ seng¹ tien³ — one is Tien³ tien³ seng¹ — one is P'en¹-hu²-lu²-pa⁴ — one is Pa⁴-hu²-lu²-pen¹ — Ch'ing² t'ou² leng⁴ can strike the musical stone — Leng⁴ t'ou² ch'ing¹ can play the pipe — Seng¹-seng¹-tien³ can play the flute — Tien³ tien³ seng¹ can strike the bell — Pen¹-hu²-lu²-pa⁴ can recite a sermon — and Pa⁴-hu²-lu²pen¹ can read the sacred books.

LXVIII

雉 雞 翎
抱 馬 城

馬 城 開
丫 頭 小 子 送 馬 來

NOTES

The military officers in the preceding dynasties used to wear on their hats feathers of the ringed pheasant (*Phasianus torquatus*) called 雉雞翎 chih⁴ chi¹ ling². The boys of the present day like to ape these old fashions and stick on their hats some cock feathers, which they suppose to be those of the pheasant. Then some of them have a pasteboard horse's head, and horse's rump; the first they tie to the stomach, the other to the back, and their infantile imagination is quite satisfied, as they gallop here and there singing these verses the meaning of which is very doubtful. The pasteboard horse has inside a frame of bamboo sticks and is called 竹馬 chu² ma³.

TRANSLATION

With ringed pheasant feathers — I gallop to the horse city — the city opens the gate — and girls and boys come out leading a horse for me.

LXIX

藍 靛 廠
四 角 兒 方

宮門口緊對着六郎莊
羅鍋兒橋怎麼那麼高
香山跑馬好熱鬧
金山銀山萬壽山
皇上求雨黑龍潭

NOTES

This song has no other aim then that of collecting names of places in Peking and near Peking. 藍靛廠 lan² tien¹ ch'ang³ the indigo factory, name of a place near Ta-chung-ssu; the ground is now occupied by military quarters for bannermen. 宮門口 kung¹ men² k'ou³, is the name of a street near the P'ing-tse-men. 六郎莊 liu⁴ lang² chuang¹ "the Liou⁴ lang²'s" farm. A place to the South of Yüan²-ming²-yüan². As a matter of fact the Kung¹ men² k'ou³ street and this farm cannot face one another because the street is inside of the city and the farm is in the Hai³-tien⁴. 羅鍋橋 luo² kuo¹ ch'iao², the hunchbacked bridge in Yüan²-ming²-yüan² (see song N° 34). 香山 hsiang¹ shan¹ "perfumed mountains" hills near Peking. 跑馬 p'ao³ ma³, the place in which military men train themselves to shoot arrows whilst galloping on horseback. 金山 chin¹ shan¹, gold mountain, name of another hill in the neighbourhood of Peking. 萬壽山 uan⁴ shou⁴ shan¹, a favourite imperial villa on a hill near Peking. It was once permissible to visit the grounds but now foreigners are no longer admitted. 求雨 ch'iu² yü³ to pray for rain, as the

Emperor in time of drought does himself or by deputy, according to the gravity of the situation. 黑龍潭 hei¹ lung² t'an¹, a temple near Peking, so called because in its grounds there is a pool where a black dragon is supposed to live. The Temple is a Government one and in time of drought imperial kins are sent there to pray for rain. In this small song there is no syntaxis; the names are huddled together without distinction or explanation. The last phrase in order to express correctly the sense, ought to say in the simplest form 皇上爲求雨遣官到黑龍潭 huang² shang⁴ wei¹ ch'iu² yü³ ch'ien³ kuan¹ tao⁴ hei¹ lung²t'an¹. The chinese original phrase could however be translated " and the temple of Hei-lung-t'an where the Emperor (goes to pray for rain or) sends people to pray for rain". As a matter of fact from Ch'ien² lung² till now no Emporor has gone there in person to pray for rain. He prays now for it in the 大高殿 ta¹ kao¹ tien⁴, the very high hall, in the interior of the Palace.

LXX

風來咯
雨來咯
老和尙背了鼓來咯

NOTES

When a storm is coming on with wind, rain,

and thunders Pekinese boys say these words. The thunder is supposed to be produced by the striking of a big drum like those which the wandering priests take round with them.

TRANSLATION

The wind has come — the rain has come — the old priest with the drum on his back has come.

LXXI

高高山上一顆蒿
兩個禿子去耍刀
兩把刀尖兒落在葫蘆兒上
一個葫蘆兩扇瓢

NOTES

一顆蒿 i¹ k'o¹ hao¹, a stem of *artemisia*. This 蒿 is for 香蒿 hsiang¹ hao¹. 禿子 t'u¹-tzŭ, small boys, as explained before. 耍刀 shua³ tao¹, to fence, to play with swords. 兩扇瓢, two gourd ladles-a gourd cut in the middle forms two ladles, used by poor people to put the rice in. The vulgar numeral is not 扇 but 個 ko⁴.

TRANSLATION

On a very high mountain there is a stem of Artemisia — two boys fence with swords — the two sword points fell on a calabash — and from a calabash were made two ladles.

LXXII

香爐兒
瓦燈臺
爺爺兒娶了個奶奶兒來
不梳頭
不作活
嘴饞手懶竟愛喝
爺爺兒沒法兒治
氣的竟哆嗦
說我打你這個拙老婆

NOTES

The first two verses are the ordinary t'ou²-tzu without any reference to what follows. 香爐兒 hsiang¹ lu² 'r, a metal or clay vessel to burn incense before the Gods; it means literally perfume-stove. 瓦燈臺 ua³ teng¹ t'ai², a sort of earthenware oil-lamp used in very poor houses. 氣的 ch'i⁴-ti, he is so irritated. 哆嗦 tuo¹ suo¹, to tremble, to shake with anger.

TRANSLATION

An incense-stove and an earthenware lamp —

the gentleman has married a lady — who does not comb her hair — does not work — is gluttonous and lazy and likes nothing but drinking — the husband has no way of correcting her — and is so angry that he trembles — and says: I will beat you stupid old woman!

LXXIII

小妞兒　　錐幫子兒
坐椅子兒　　衲底子兒

NOTES

Girls in poor families make their own shoes. 錐幫子 chui¹ pang¹ tzü, to bore with an awl holes into the cloth for binding it to the sole. 衲底子 na⁴ ti³-tzü, to beat the sole to harden it. The sole is made of felt.

TRANSLATION

The little girl — is sitting on the chair — bores the sides of the shoe — and beats the sole of the shoe.

LXXIV

爺爺抱孫子
坐在波棱蓋兒

羊肉包子蘸醋蒜兒
吃完了撒嬌兒
過來打你爺爺三嘴巴兒

NOTES

蘸 chan⁴, to dip in, said of a brush in the ink, or of meat in the sauce. 醋蒜兒 ts'u⁴ suan¹ 'r, sort of sauce made of vinegar and bits of garlic. 撒嬌兒 sa¹ chiao¹ 'r, to gambol, to tease, said of spoilt children. 嘴巴 tsuei³ pa¹, a blow in the face.

TRANSLATION

The grandfather embraces his grandson — who sits on his knees — (the grandfather says) here are meat-balls to dip in vinegar sauce — when you have finished eating you will be saucy — and will come over to hit your grandfather three blows in the face.

LXXV

小脚兒娘
愛吃糖
沒錢兒買
搬着小脚兒哭一場

NOTES

搬脚 pan¹ chiao³, to sit down with crossed legs holding the feet in the hands. Children often sit so when disappointed and weeping.

TRANSLATION.

The little lady with the small feet — likes to eat sugar — but has no money to buy it — and sits crosslegged and weeps for a good while.

LXXVI

高髙山上一座樓
兩個姑娘去梳頭
大姐梳的盤龍髻
二姐梳的賽花樓
三姐梳的沒梳
一梳梳了個獅子滾繡毬
大姐姐坐的是金板凳
二姐姐坐的是銀板凳
剩下三姐沒的坐
一坐坐在一盤磨
大姐抱着個金娃子
二姐抱着個銀娃子

三姐沒得抱
一抱抱着個樹磕杈

NOTES

盤龍髻 p'an² lung² chi⁴, sort of women's head dress; literally coiled dragon chignon. 賽花樓 sai⁴ hua¹ lou², another sort of head dress very high and adorned with flowers; it means literally "tower which emulate the flowers". 獅子滾繡毬 shih¹ tzǐ kun³ hsiou⁴ ch'iu², "a lion who rolls an embroidered ball" sort of amusement in the fairs. Two men dress themselves as lions and then fight, in the same time pushing with the feet a large embroidered ball. Here the phrase is used in the meaning of "confused, not well done, ruffled". — 盤磨 i¹ p'an² muo⁴, a mill-stone.

TRANSLATION

On a very high mountain there is a high tower — two girls go there to comb their hair — the eldest sister combs her hair into a "coiled dragon chignon" — The second sister combs her hair into a "rivalling flowers tower chignon" — the third sister has no other way of combing her hair — and combs it in a ruffled way — the first sister sits on a golden stool — the second sister sits on a silver stool — there remains the third sister who has no room to sit — and sits on a stone-mill — the first sister folds in her arms a golden baby — the second sister folds in her arms a silver baby — the third sister has nothing to fold in the arms — and folds a forked branch.

LXXVII

嗩 嗩
王 八 是 你 哥 哥
駱 駝 駱 駝 拜 拜
王 八 是 你 太 太
駱 駝 駱 駝 抽 鼻 兒
王 八 是 你 小 姨 兒

NOTES

Pekinese boys address these words to camels, which are well tempered enough not to take any notice of them. 嗩嗩 so¹ so¹, signal given to the camels to make them kneel down, to receive the load on their back. The word is probably derived from the word *sok* used by Mongol camel drivers. The same word is however used to call a dog to come. 拜拜 pai⁴ pai⁴, to salute as women do; here the words refer to the awkward movement of the camels when kneeling down. 抽鼻兒 ch'ou¹ pi² 'r, to sniff, as camels use to do. 小姨兒 hsiao³ i² 'r, a man's wife's younger sister.

TRANSLATION

Camel, camel, kneel down — a turtle is your older brother — camel, camel, make a salute — a turtle is your wife — camel, camel, sniff — a turtle is your sister-in-law.

LXXVIII

七八
你媽小腳兒開黃花
你媽
我媽
左一盤兒
右一盤兒
你媽肚子裏有小孩兒
多大了
曾走了
你媽肚子裏又有了

NOTES

Two things are to be observed in the first two verses. Apparently there is nothing wrong in them but it is quite the contrary. Ladies generally avoid pronouncing in succession the numbers seven ch'i¹ and eight pa¹, because, these two syllabes put together, give a sound very similar to that of an equivocal word largely spoken by Chinamen. Now in this case the two syllabes are separated but no Chinese will fail to understand the meaning of it, so much more that translating the numerals simply as they are, would convey no meaning in the two first verses. Again-the word 八 that is to say the number eight, has been chosen by Chinese to mean what in higher style would be called 玉門 yü⁴ men². Therefore the meaning of the second verse cannot be an edifying one. 開黃花, k'ai¹ huang² hua¹, "to open yellow flowers" it seems that in Pekinese slang a "yellow flower foot" means a small foot. 一盤兒 i¹ p'an² 'r, a tour, a walk.

TRANSLATION

Your mother "seven" — your mother "eight" — your mother has small feet — a tour to the left — and a tour to the right — your mother is in a family way — "how old is the baby"? — "he can walk" — your mother is again in a family way.

LXXIX

桃樹葉兒尖
荷花葉兒圓
梔子開花兒喚牡丹
仙人掌手拿三棱兒草
淑氣花開挨了一頓霸王鞭

NOTES

仙人掌 hsien¹ jen² chang, a cactus, (*Opuntia Dillenii*). 三棱草 san¹ leng² ts'ao³, lit. "grass with three edges" a three-cornered sedge *(Cyperus)*. 淑氣花 shu² ch'i¹ hua¹, called in vulgar language 蜀角 shou² chiao⁴ (the original pronunciation and tones ought to be shu³ chiao³), the hollyhock (lat. *Althæa rosea*). 霸王鞭 pa⁴ uang² pien¹, tyrant's whip, a sort of cactus, called so because of its resemblance to an iron whip property of a king of the Ch'u 楚 kingdom, renowned for his bodily strength, named 項羽 Hsiang⁴ yū³. In the last verse the phrase has a double meaning as 挨一頓鞭 ai² i¹ tun⁴ pien¹, means to receive a number of whip blows.

TRANSLATION

The peach tree leaves are pointed — the lotus leaves are round — the gardenia opens its flowers and calls the peony tree flower — the cactus (the wise man's palm) holds in its hands the three cornered sedge — the hollyhock flower opens and receives a good many blows from the "tyrant's whip".

LXXX

小小子兒
拿倒錘兒

兒
門子兒
扇椅子兒
兩漆子兒
屋子兒脚搭
怯椁着脚
壺子兒
開仙登滿篋橡根大猪上下聲南大蕉扇子蚊子兒
開八足水洗四嫩八燒天撤叫上聽芭打

人兒
道席兒
個素席兒
是擺飽了
名景
有韭菜
茶菜兒
嫩仁兒
蝦子兒
鴨兒
娘是
席擺
娘吃

NOTES

拿倒 na² tao⁴, to hold a thing just in the opposite way form that in which it ought to be held, for instance taking a sword by the point. 錘 ch'ui², a toy for boys which imitates an ancient weapon to be seen now only on the theatres, it is formed of a large ball of iron to which is attached a handle, and can be compared to our mace used in the middle ages. 怯屋子 ch'ie⁴ wu¹ tzŭ, a common, plain room, as of labourers in the fields. 八仙棹子 pa¹ hsien¹ chuo¹ tzŭ, a table for eight persons. 漆椅子 ch'i¹ i³ tzŭ, lacquered chairs. 脚搭子 chiao³ ta¹ tzǔ, a small four-legged stool to lay the feet on. 鑹子 ts'uan¹ tzǔ, very vulgar name for a kettle. 名景 ming² ching³, fame, renown. 嫩根兒 nen¹ ken¹'r, with delicate stems. 韭菜 chiou³ ts'ai⁴, leeks. 八大 pa¹ ta¹ instead of 八大碗 pa¹ ta¹ wan³, the eight entries in a good chinese dinner. The verse is very laconic. 燴蝦仁兒 huei¹ hsia¹ jen²'r, shrimp pulp with sauce. 天上大娘 t'ien¹ shang⁴ ta¹ niang², a fairy in heaven, but here very probably a term of flattery for a nun. 道人兒 tao⁴ jen²'r, said also in relation to above, a person who has reached the perfection of reason, a holy person. 葷席 hun¹ hsi², a dinner comprising meat and food, which persons in monastic life should abstain from eating. 南台 nan² t'ai², the theatre placed on the Southern side. 芭蕉 pa¹ chiao¹, palm tree. 打蚊子 ta³ uen²-tzǔ, to drive away the sandflies.

TRANSLATION

The small boy — holding the mace by the head — opens the two leaves of the door of the plain room — (inside there are) one table for eight people and varnished chairs — he leans his feet on a small footstool — the tea pot is overfilled with water — and washes the kettle — four sorts of food are there spread out — delicate leeks with delicate stems — and eight plates with sauced shrimp pulp — pork with sauce and roasted duck — (the nun) like the great lady in heaven is a holy person — and she has the common food removed and vegetable food prepared — people call out: the great lady has eaten to fullness — and goes to the Southern stage — to see the play — and with a palm-leaf fan — strikes away the mosquitoes.

LXXXI

高高山上一顆蔴
有個吉了兒往上爬
我問吉了兒爬怎的
他說渴了要吃蔴

NOTES

吉了兒 chi² liao³'r, the cicada, correctly written 蟬蟟兒. 怎的 tsen³ ti, antiquated form for 怎麽着 tsem³ mo cho, how? why? 吃蔴 ch'ih¹ ma², to eat hemp, a curious way of letting thirst pass away.

TRANSLATION

On a very high mountain there is a stem of hemp — there is a cicada who creeps on it — I ask the cicada, why do you creep on? — and she says: I am thirsty and want to eat hemp.

LXXXII

好熱天兒
掛竹簾兒

歪脖兒樹底下
有個妞兒哄着我頑兒
穿着一件大紅坎肩兒
沒有沿邊兒
梳油頭
別玉簪兒
左手拿着玉花籃兒
右手拿着梔子茉莉串枝蓮兒

NOTES

歪脖兒樹 uai¹ puo²'r shu⁴, "trees with a crooked neck" crooked trees. 大紅 ta⁴ hung², deep red. 沿邊兒 yen² pien¹'r, coloured border of ladies dresses. 油頭 iu² t'ou² a hairdress combed with odorous oil. 別 pie², there is no particular character for the meaning; it means to wear pins in the hair as women do. 花籃兒 hua¹ lan²'r, a flower basket.

TRANSLATION

What a hot day — set up the bamboo curtain! — under the crooked trees — there is a small girl who plays and jests with me — she wears a deep red waistcoat — without coloured border — she has combed her hair with oil — and has stuck jade pins into her hair — in the left hand she helds a flower basket — and in the right hand she helds gardenias, jasmine and wild lotus flowers.

LXXXIII

羊巴巴蛋兒
用腳撮
你是兄來我是哥
打壺酒兒偺們倆人喝
喝醉了
打老婆
吹鼻兒打鼓再娶一個

NOTES

The beginning of this song is nasty but I could not cut it off the song. 羊巴巴蛋兒 yang² pa³ pa³ tan'r, goat dung — 打壺酒兒 ta³ hu² chiou³, to go to buy a bottle of wine. 鼻兒 pi²'r, the mouth of a flute, therefore 吹鼻兒 ch'ui¹ pi²'r, means to play the flute or other wind instrument. This phrase alludes to the band of players which accompanies the chair of a bride.

TRANSLATION

Goat's dung — crushed by the foot — you are my second brother and I am your first brother — go and buy a bottle of wine; we will both drink it — when I am drunk — I will beat my wife — and then with flute-players and drummers I will marry another.

LXXXIV

兒
廟兒
小廟兒
個神道兒
有個帽兒
上着草罩兒
山住藍皮套兒
高頭穿草要小抬轎兒
高裏穿繫個小鬼兒
兒哇嗚哇吹號兒
兩解個南小來嗚了青年少兒
腰四小鬼提一春元實兩吊兒
鬼兒抱還罷了
懷懷個抱抱兒
懷我兒兒
給我把燒你的小廟兒
不給火花聽心好惱
點把兒兒聞發票兒兒
灰兒道花鬼年少兒
神聲兒小春少少兒
叫拿青青年少泡兒
快的青春冒兒
嚇郎咕郎嘟

NOTES

罩兒 chao⁴'r, very thin overcoat which the Chinese

wear over their clothes. 草要兒 ts'ao³ yao⁴'r, sort of rope made of dry grass to bind vegetables together, and in this case as a girdle. 温兒哇 weur¹ wa¹, imitates the sound of the trumpet. 吹號 for 吹號筒 ch'ui¹ hao⁴ t'ung³, to blow the trumpet. 青春 ch'ing¹ ch'un, the pure spring, the flower of life, youth. 千張 ch'ien¹ chang¹, a paper ladder burned in ceremonies in order to give the spirits a way to ascend to heaven. 元寶兩吊 yüan² pao³ liang³ tiao⁴, two strings of paper money, resembling the silver yüan-pao, which the Chinese burn for their dead and in other offerings. 懷抱兒 huai² pao⁴'r, something to carry in the bosom, a child. 一把火 i¹ pa⁴ huo³, a bundle of combustible matter for obtaining a fire. 灰兒花兒 hui¹'r hua¹'r, wants to imitate the noise of a conflagration. 發票 fa¹ p'iao⁴, to issue a warrant to arrest a man. 冐泡兒 mao⁴ p'ao⁴'r, to gasp and let air out of the mouth as fish does when just taken out of the water; that is said to show the agonizing fear of the young girl. 咕嘟咕嘟 ku¹ tu¹ ku¹ tu¹, imitates the gurgling round of the air gasping out of the throat.

TRANSLATION

On a very high mountain — there is a small temple — inside is sitting a holy man — who wears on his head a dry grass hat — and on his body an azure cloak — and on his legs skin leggings — and round his waist a grass rope for girdle — four small devils bear the chair — two small devils blow the trumpet — from the South has come a young girl in the bloom of life — who has in her hands a paper ladder and paper money — she enters the temple — to pray for a child — (she says:) give me a child and it shall be all right — if you do not give me a child — I will make a fire — and burn your small temple — the holy man hearing this is very much angry — and calls for the small devils to issue a warrant of arrest — (saying) quickly apprehend this young woman in the bloom of life, — but the young woman in the bloom of life is so scared that she gasps for breath.

LXXXV

有個妞兒不害羞
管着賣花的叫舅舅
舅舅舅舅給我一朵紅石榴
懷裏揣
袖裏袖
利利拉拉一大溜

NOTES

揣 ch'uai, means to feel, to grope, and also to hide in the bosom, as Chinese do because of their not having pockets. 袖 hsiou⁴, a sleeve, and also, to place in the sleeve 利利拉拉 li⁴ li⁴ la¹ la¹ — without interruption-without end. 一大溜 i¹ ta⁴ liu⁴, a great row a great number of.

TRANSLATION

There is a small girl who does not feel ashamed — and calls the flower seller her own uncle — uncle, uncle give me a flower of the red pomegranate — I will put it in my bosom — I will put it in my sleeve — and all the ground shall be strown with flowers.

LXXXVI

高姓本兒禿小個有
燒女香把五十一初
女毛兒香香一燒家人
毛上長爲爲燒家禿
　　長天三子到
　　毛毛香香了又
　　　爺架火了爺拿燒香袍燒又
　　了掉冲怒三三掛到
　　燒爺冲開瓢了袍搬
　　　見就　一了老
　　　大刀　倒爺
　　　　　　爺拿
　　　　　　起

NOTES

The Chinese are accustomed to burn incense on the first and fifteenth of a month. 爲長毛 uei⁴ chang⁴ mao², to make the hair grow. 掛袍 kua¹ p'ao², "to put on Buddha's body a jacket". Some people who want to get a favour from the Divinity, to soothe him, buy a silk or satin jacket which they themselves put on his body. 搬倒了 pan¹ tao³ la, he upset the God. 老爺 lao³ ye², Mister, Sir, gentleman, here it is instead of 關老爺 kuan¹ lao³ ye², the God of war. 架 chia⁴, to lean the object on a stand, here in order to burn it completely. 冲冲怒 ch'ung¹ ch'ung¹ nu⁴, in great irritation.

TRANSLATION.

There was a small bald-headed man, whose name was Kao — who went to burn incense on the first and on the fifteenth — people burn incense to get a son or a daughter — but the baldheaded man burns incense to make his hair grow — after three days the hair was growing — and he burns incense — and dresses the God with a new jacket — after three days the hair fell off — and he upset the Kuanti statue and placed him against a stand to burn him — But Kuanti seeing that, was awfully irritated — he took up his great halberd and split the man's calebash (head) into two ladles.

LXXXVII

兒 站 立 立 立 立
　　　兒 沿 河 上
兒 半 兩 劈 猪 個 一
　　　兒 半 一 你
　　　兒 半 一 我
兒 菜 酒 就 酒 打

NOTES

The first word li⁴ is reapeted four times for the sake of the rhythm. 就酒菜兒 chiou⁴ chiou³ ts'ai⁴'r, to accompan ythe food which is generally taken whilst drinking wine; here it alludes to the pig's head..

TRANSLATION

I top here — go on the banks of the river — of a pig's head we will make two portions — you will get a half — and I will get a half — and we will go and buy wine to suit the wine-food.

LXXXVIII

鑼鍋兒橋
萬壽山
鎮海銅牛在上邊
賣豆腐腦兒的
喝喝連連在海淀

NOTES

This song is not very intelligible; names of places are put together without any apparent reason. 鎮 chen⁴, to protect against bad luck and danger. 鎮物 chen⁴ u⁴, an object which counteracts evil influences. The brass ox which is spoken of here is on the shore of the lake k'un¹ ming² hu² and is there to oppose the danger which chinese believe would arise from the overflowing of the lake. In the lake there is supposed to be a 海眼 hai³ yen³, that is to say a "sea-eye" a hole in the bottom of the lake which communicates with the sea, and out of which all the sea water would rise and overflow the country. The lake 昆明湖 k'un¹ ming² hu² is in the Haitien in the neighbourhood of Peking. 在上邊 tzai⁴ shang⁴ pien¹, on the shore. 豆腐腦 tou⁴ fu³ nao³, sort of bean-curd. 喝喝 ho¹ ho¹, cries of vendors in the street. 連連 lien² lien², without interruption.

TRANSLATION

The hunchback bridge — Wan-shou-shan — the brass oxen on the shore, which protects the country from the sea water — the vendors of bean curd — go along crying their ware without interruption.

———

LXXXIX

黑老婆兒
滿地滾
嗔着他男人不買粉
買了粉他不搽
嗔着他男人不買蔴
買了蔴他不打
嗔着他男人不買馬
買了馬他不餵
嗔着他男人不買櫃
買了櫃他不盛

嗔着他男人不買繩
買了繩他上弔
嚇了他男人一大跳

NOTES

滿地滾 man³ ti⁴ kun³, rolls all over the ground. 嗔着 ch'en¹ cho², speaking angrily, scolding. 打蔴 ta³ ma², to beat the hemp, to take away the bark from the stems. 盛 here read ch'eng², to fill something with, to put, to place in. 上弔 shang⁴ tiao⁴, to hang oneself.

TRANSLATION

The old brown woman — rolls herself all over the ground — scolding because her husband does not buy cosmetic for her — but when he has bought cosmetic then she does not use it — scolding because her husband does not buy hemp for her — when he has bought hemp, then she does not thrash it — scolding because her husband does not buy a horse — when he has bought a horse, she does not feed it — scolding because her husband does not buy a wardrobe — when he has bought the wardrobe, she does not puts her things there — scolding because her husband has not bought a cord — when he has bought a cord, she hangs herself — and frightens her husband to death.

XC

小小子兒
胖咕圖墪兒
骼臂上戴着個金鐲子兒
身穿紅兜肚綠褲子兒
腦袋瓜兒梳着個歪毛兒
一笑倆酒窩
一走一哆嗦
拉着姐姐偕們買果子

NOTES

胖咕圖墪兒 p'ang¹ ku¹ lun¹ tun¹'r, fat and round, said of a child. 兜肚 tou¹ tu⁴, a covering for the stomach worn by children. 腦袋瓜兒 nao³ tai⁴ kua¹'r, the head, the skull, a jocular expression. 歪毛兒 uai¹ mao² 'r, a round tuft of hair which small boys wear either on the right or on the left of the head. 酒窩兒 chiu³ uo¹'r, dimples in the cheek.

TRANSLATION

The very little boy — is round and fat — he wears a gold bracelet on his arm — and wears a red stomach protector and green trowsers — on his head he wears a tuft of hair — when he laughs two dimples appear on his cheeks — when he walks all his body trembles — and taking the elder sister by the hand says: elder sister, let us go and buy fruit.

XCI

黃城根兒
一溜門兒
門口兒站着個小妞人兒
有個意思兒
白布汗褟兒藍布褲子兒
耳朶上戴着排環墜
頭上梳的是大抓髻兒
搽着胭兒
抹着粉兒
誰是我的小女婿兒

NOTES

皇城 huang² ch'eng², the wall which goes round the imperial city. 城根兒 ch'eng² ken¹'r, near the wall, opposite to it. 妞人兒 niu¹-jen², rather affected for the sake of rhyme instead of the simple 妞兒 niu¹'r. 有個意思兒 iou³ ko⁴ i⁴ ssu⁴'r, there is a thought, it is amusing pleasant to look at it and to think of it. 排環墜兒 p'ai² huan² chuei⁴'r, a sort of earrings for women. 搽胭 ch'a¹ yen¹, to rub rose cosmetic on the cheeks or on the palms of the hands. 抹粉 muo³ fen³, to rub white cosmetic powder on the cheeks. 小女婿兒 hsiao³ nu³ hsü⁴, a small son-in-law, said to a girl to mean her bridegroom.

TRANSLATION

Near the wall of the imperial town — there is

a row of doors — near a door there stands a small girl — she is really nice — with a shirt of white cloth and trowsers of blue cloth — she wears round earrings — and has a great chignon on her head — on the face she has rubbed red powder — and white powder — who shall be my bittle bridegroom?

XCII

簷蝙蝠　　你是奶奶兒
穿花鞋　　我是爺

NOTES

The first two verses are the common introduction without definite meaning. 簷蝙蝠 the bat is called in suhua yen¹ pien⁴ hu³, but the regular pronunciation ought to be yen² pien⁴ fu². As to the fact of wearing embroidered shoes, the chinese explain as follows: sometimes in order to catch a bat, a shoe is thrown in the air, and the bat himself runs into the shoe and so falls to the ground and is taken. Very likely the need of a rhyme has forced in the whole phrase.

TRANSLATION

The bat — wears embroidered shoes — you are a wife — and I am a husband.

XCIII

老太太叫貓
花兒花兒花兒狐狸喲
我們的貓有名兒
鞭打繡球金鑲玉
雪裏送炭四個銀蹄
有人要偷了我們的貓兒去
抽了你的筋來
剝了你的皮

NOTES

花兒花兒 hua¹'r hua¹'r, is equivalent to the english puss! puss! to call a cat. 花兒狐狸 hua¹'r hu² li² striped fox-the name of one of the cats belonging to the lady. 鞭打繡球 pien¹ ta³ hsiou⁴ ch'iu², means literally "a whip that beats the embroidered ball". The coats of cats have different curious names to distinguish them. This phrase means a cat which has a black tail and a black spot on the forehead, meaning that with his long black tail (the whip) he strikes the black spot on the forehead (the embroidered ball). 金鑲玉 chin¹ hsiang¹ yü⁴, another name for a cat's coat "jade inlaid with gold" a cat with a white coat with yellow spots. 雪裏送炭 hsüe³ li³ sung⁴ t'an⁴, another name, literally explained "coal sent in the snow" a black coat with four white paws. 銀蹄 in²-t'i², a silver hoof, said of white hoofs and paws.

TRANSLATION

The old lady calls the cat — puss, puss! Fox — our cats have all a name — (there is) " the whip that beats the embroidered ball" and " jade inlaid with gold " — and more " coal brought in the snow " with four white paws — if there is a man who wants to steal away my cat — I will draw out your muscles — and peel away your skin.

XCIV

怕蠟燭害了
他媽兒罷去
兒孩子一聲我滾出不回家
媽個兒摔了
就燈
我頂着兒
見着油腳
兒不瞧下了跑
椒辣爸地流前還挨
秦麼爸在洗往子臭烟
怎我怕薇說袋茶
小跪還媽參了是過碗我
我脫媽爹過袋我媽
要要往的爸叫
裝遞樂爸太太生氣
我老再從今兒永遠

NOTES

This song is supposed to be sung by a small boy who innocently relates the strife between father and mother. In China although the family laws are severe and different from ours, yet there exists a sufficient number of henpecked husbands. A number of anecdotes regarding uxorious husbands are currently spread. 秦椒 ch'in² chiao¹, chillies (lat. *Capsicum annuum*); very likely here the house wife is not wrongly likened to the chillies. 爸爸 pa⁴ pa⁴, common appellation for father, and the same as our papa. 頂着燈 ting³-cho¹-teng¹, bearing a lamp on the head; a henpecked husband is jestingly supposed to kneel down before his wife, who orders him as a punishment to stay a long time in that position, with an oil-lamp on his head. So the husband must endure the pain of being scalded by the oil that drops down from the lamp and runs on his back. This notion is so generally known and jested about that one of the must common tricks to produce general hilarity is to alarm a friend by saying he has got oil-stains on his back. Everybody understands what fictions that alludes to. 油 iu², for oil is intended here the product of the melting of wax. 一袋烟 i¹ tai⁴ yen¹, a pipe filled with tobacco. 孩兒他媽 hai²'r t'a¹ ma¹, "the children's mother" title given by the husband to a wife who has born children to him. The wife in her turn calls the husband 孩兒他爸爸 hai²'r t'a¹ pa¹ pa¹, the children's father. Two abridged phrases for that are 他媽 and 他爹.

TRANSLATION

The small chillies — how could they not be bitter? — when my father catches sight of my mother, he is afraid — he kneels down with a lamp on his head, — and is also afraid lest the oil should run down, or the candle should fall — when my mother wants to wash her feet — my father runs forward — when he has taken down the socks he says that it is scented — if he says it is bad smelling he gets a slap on the face — when he has filled her pipe — and handed over to her a cup of tea — my mother is so delighted that she shows her teeth — my father has once called her : o mother of my children — old lady, forgive me, now — if you are going to get angry again, I will roll away — and from now henceforward I will never come back home.

XCV

蒿 子 燈　　今 兒 點
荷 葉 燈　　明 兒 個 扔

NOTES

On the fifteenth day of the seventh moon is celebrated the Feast of the Spirits 中元節 chung¹ yüan² chie². In the evening many lanterns are lighted on the streets. 蒿子燈 hao¹ tzǔ³ teng¹, it is not a lantern but a whole plant of artemisia on the branches of which incense sticks are bound and then lighted.

荷葉燈 ho² ye⁴ teng¹, another lantern formed of a leaf of lotus on which a candle has been fixed.

TRANSLATION

The artemisia lantern — and the lotus-lantern — to day they are lighted — and to-morrow they are thrown away.

XCVI

他媽兒三小
媽砣房頂
眼摳窩
脖長挺
穿着一件破袷襖
窟窿兒大
補丁多
渾身的鈕子沒有兩個
告訴你媽嫁了我罷
又得吃來又得喝

NOTES

頂 ting³, to reach with the head. 房砣 fang² t'uo², the principal beam in the roof. 摳 k'ou¹ means here sunken, deep and 窩摳眼 uo¹ k'ou¹ yen³, sunken eyes. 挺 t'ing³, character used to form the superlative in very common language, used instead of 頂 ting³.

袲襺 tuo³ luo², sort of old dress consisting of a long gown with a high collar, worn in winter time.
補丁 pu³ ting¹, patches. A chinese coat has never more than six buttons.

TRANSLATION

Sar's mother — is as tall as the roof — has sunken eyes — and a very long neck — she wears a broken overcoat — with big holes — and many patches — on her whole person there are not even two buttons — now, tell your mother to marry me! — she will get food and drink.

XCVII

小耗子兒　　偷油吃
上燈台　　　下不來

TRANSLATION

The small mouse — has climbed up the candlestick — to steal oil to eat — and now cannot come down.

XCVIII

兩枝蠟
一股香
二十三日祭竈王
一碟兒草料

永上天堂
一碗水下地
潑在地下把頭叩
當家的過來响叮噹
三聲爆竹
竈王爺
囘來罷囘來罷
給你留着關東糖

NOTES

This song speaks about the ceremony for the God of the stove on the 23ᵈ day of the twelfth moon. Before the God's picture incense is burning and on the table there is a dish containing water, and one with grass which is supposed to serve for the God's horse. The water then is thrown to the ground and the grass in the air. That means the end of this ceremony. 當家的 tang¹ chia¹ ti, the oldest man in the family who is called to perform the sacrifices and all religious ceremonies. 天堂 t'ien¹ t'ang², the Heavenly hall, the paradise. 爆竹 p'ao⁴ chu², fire crackers. 响叮噹 hsiang³ ting¹ tang¹, the noise is ting-tang; 關東糖 kuan¹-tung¹ t'ang², Manchurian sugar. The Chinese offer sugar to this God, with the aim of letting his teeth stick together and so prevent him from relating to Heaven all the inconvenience and misdeed he had occasion to see in the family during twelve months; with this hope, the Chinese merrily begin their New-year.

TRANSLATION

Two candles — a bundle of incense sticks — on the 23ᵈ day it is sacrificed to the God of the hearth — there is a dish full of grass — and a dish full of water — when the water is thrown on the ground the God ascends to Heaven — the eldest of the family comes over and knocks his head on the ground — then three volleys of crackers with a great noise — God of the hearth — come back! come back! — we keep for you Manchurian sugar.

XCIX

八仙棹兒
四角兒方
盤子碗兒擺在中央
燒猪燒鴨子東坡肉
保府帶來的八寶香腸

NOTES

四角兒 ssu⁴ chiao⁰'r, with four corners. 中央 chung yang¹, in the middle-the word yang¹ is pronounced vulgarly-yang². 東坡肉 tung¹ p'uo¹ jou⁴, sort of meat prepared in a special way as directed by a certain old literary man who was a great authority also on kitchen matters. His name was 蘇軾 Su¹-shih⁴ and his surname, hao, was Tung p'uo¹. 保府 Pao³-fu³ is instead of 保定府 Pao³ ting⁴ fu³, the head prefecture in the Chih-li province. 八寶香腸 pa¹ pao³ hsiang¹ ch'ang² " the odorous sausages with eight treasures " a sort of sausages made of pork stuffed into chicken's intestines. The eight treasures alluded to are the spices, aromas which are in the stuff. These sausages come from Pao-ting-fu.

TRANSLATION

A table for eight persons — with four corners square — plates and cups are placed in the middle of it — roast pork, roast duck, and meat prepared à la Tung-p`uo — and sausages from Pao-ting-fu.

C

喜兒喜兒吃豆腐
小鷄兒過來嗛把穀
狗兒汪汪要看家
貓兒過來會撲鼠

NOTES

喜兒 hsi³'r stands for 喜雀 hsi³ ch'iao³, the magpie. 嗛 ch'ien¹, to peck. 汪汪 uang¹ uang¹, imitates the noise of barking. 撲鼠 p'u¹ shu³, to rush on mice, to catch mice as cats do. These words are repeated by children when they catch sight of magpies.

TRANSLATION

The magpie, the magpie eats beancurd — the chicken comes over and pecks a handful of grain —

the dog barks and wants to look after the house —
the cat comes over and wants to catch the mice.

CI

喜兒喜兒買豆腐
該我的錢
臘月二十五

NOTES

Chinese accounts and debts are paid at the end of every quarter and the great bulk of money accounts ought to be paid, in the 12th month from the 25th day to the 30th at midnight.

TRANSLATION

The magpie, the magpie buys beancurd — those who owe me money — (I shall see them) on the 25th day of the 12th moon.

CII

顧不得一時睡着
你槓槍
我揹鎗
上南洼
刨元寶

包䐡
蒲䐡裏
大元寶
個望銀兒
出包銀鑽兒
刨蒲寶鑽脊子
刨着元鋼大珊瑚
一隔金金兩珊瑚要買人要買房子要買驢要開當鋪要開錢桌兒東邊兒摸西邊兒摸摸了個青頭愣的螢的
高燒
兩丈跑火倒力兒潮保
樹逃怕槽眼子沒人兒
子怕房當鋪錢桌兒摸摸個青頭愣的蠍子
人買買驢開開邊邊了個愣的我鬼哭神嚎

NOTES

The song relates a dream. 顧不得 ku⁴ pu⁴ to², without a perceiving it; insensibly. 鎬 kao³, said also 钁頭 chüe³ t'ou², a hoe. The first character is not noted in dictionaries. 刨 p'ao², to dig the ground with a hoe. 蒲包 p'u² pao¹, a bundle made of rushes. 金鋼石 chin¹ kang¹ shih³, the diamond. 金鋼鑽兒 chin¹ kang¹ tsuan⁴'r, the diamond-pointed awl used by menders of crockery. 倒槽 tao³ ts'ao², said of animals "to die near the manger, in the stable". 眼力兒潮 yen³ li³'r ch'ao³, lit. the strenght of the eyes is damp, that is to say we have not eyes good enough to distinguish good objects from bad ones - a faculty which is necessary in such an establishment as a pawn-shop. The word ch'ao² has also in other cases the meaning of not up to, insufficient, as in 潮銀子 ch'ao² yin² tzu, bad silver, with too much alloy. 錢桌子 ch'ien² cho¹-tzu, lit. "money-table" a bank authorized to issue small banknotes and guaranteed by other banks. 摸 muo¹, to feel with the hands, read here vulgarly ma³². 鬼哭神嚎 kuei³ k'u¹ shen² hao², "the devils weep and the spirits wail" that is "in a very painful way".

TRANSLATION

Without perceiving it in a moment I fell asleep — (I dreamed) you had shouldered a gun — and I shouldered a hoe — and went to the South morass — to dig out silver ingots — and digging we dug out a big rush wrapper — through the rush wrapper we looked in — there were gold ingots and silver ingots — and two large buckets of diamonds — and two coral trees two chang high — but if we buy servants I am afraid they would run away — if we buy houses I am afraid they would burn — if we buy an ass, I am afraid he would die near the manger — if we open a pawn-shop, we have not eyes good enough for that — if we open a money-shop, there is none who will guarantee us — but feeling for the East — and feeling for the West — I felt a big ugly scorpion — which bit me so painfully that it made me scream.

CIII

大姐
小二姐
小你拉胡琴兒　我打鐵
掙了錢兒
腰裏掖
買個蒲包兒　贐乾爹
乾爹戴着紅纓帽
乾兒穿着厚底兒鞋
走一步
格登登
扎蝴蝶兒鴨蛋青

NOTES

拉胡琴兒 la¹-hu²-ch'in²'r, to play the tartar fiddle. 打鐵 ta³ t'ie³, to beat the iron, to work the iron. 腰裏掖 yao¹ li³ye¹, to hide, to place something in the waist. — These baskets made of rushes are especially used for containing objects for gifts. 格登登 ko² teng¹ teng¹ imitates the noise of the shoes slapping on the ground. 鴨蛋青 ya¹ tan¹ ch'ing¹, of the same colour as the eggs of ducks.

TRANSLATION

You the first small young lady — and I the second small young lady — you play on the fiddle — and I will strike the iron — when we will have gained money — we will put it in the waist — we will buy a rush basket and will go to see our adopted father — Our adopted father has a red fringed hat — and our adopted mother has shoes with a thick sole — at every step — the creaking is heard — the butterflies embroidered on the shoes are of duck's egg colour.

CIV

咯
幾要了
十要娶
娘家兒龍
姑婆對兒鳳
新婆一對兒
　　一鉞斧朝天鐙
　　金瓜鞋兒
　　小紅兒夢
　　蝴蝶棹子上板凳
　　跳了

NOTES

The dragon is compared to the bridegroom and the phoenix bird to the bride. In the marriage cortege there are taken round a pair of banners on which the dragon is painted and another pair on which is painted the phoenix. 金瓜 chin¹ kua¹, gilt wood gourd stuck to the end of a pole and taken round. 鉞斧 yüo⁴ fu³, a sort of wooden axe. 朝天鐙 ch'ao² t'ien¹ teng⁴, a stirrup iron turned upside down and stuck on a pole. 小紅鞋兒 hsiao³ hung² hsie²'r, red satin shoes worn by the bride. 蝴蝶兒夢 hu² t'ier² r meng⁴, the Dream of the butterflies, name of a pattern of shoes on which butterflies are embroidered.

TRANSLATION

The bride is ten years and more — the mother-in-law wants to take her home — a pair of dragon flags — and a pair of phoenix flags — and gilt gourds, gilt axes, and reversed stirrups. — (the bride wears) small red shoes — and she jumps on the table and then on the bench.

CV

有邊兒有邊兒眞有邊兒
藍布的大衫兒
青坎肩兒
時興花兒的袴子賽糧船兒

NOTES

These words describe the toilet of a small girl. 有邊兒 iou³ pien¹'r, slang phrase which means to be very nice, to be first rate. 衫兒 shan¹'r, read here shan³'r, a summer thin bodice. 時興 shih² hsing₁, the fashion. 賽糧船兒 sai¹ liang² ch'uan²'r, bigger, larger than a ship used to bring the grain tributes.

TRANSLATION

She is first rate, first rate, really first rate! — with a great bodice of azure cloth — and a brown waistcoat — and trowsers with a new pattern, as large as a rice junk.

CVI

出了門兒好喪氣
瞧了個兔子倒憨氣
剛要拿槍打
看了一看
是個拉屎的

NOTES

In Peking, generally acknowledged to be the dirtiest city in the world, it is not an uncommon sight to see people stopping on the public streets to perform the duties of nature. The chinese do not resent it but the boys have composed these few verses which they sing loudly, when the occasion arises of insulting any one caught in the act. 好 hao³ does not mean here good but " how much "! how great ! — We have already hinted at the double meaning of the word hare in China. Here the word is not used without a reason; 倒憋氣 tao⁴ pie¹ ch'i⁴, means to draw in the breath as if preparing for an effort.

TRANSLATION

As soon as I came out of my gate, what an unauspicious sight ! — I saw a hare which was drawing in its breath — I was just going to take the gun and shoot — when looking more closely — it was a man who had been taken short !

CVII

咚咚咚
坐轎兒
一坐坐到二廟兒
二廟東
二廟西
裏頭坐着個肥公雞
哏哏哏兒
上草垛

NOTES

咚咚咚 tung¹ tung¹ tung¹, imitates the noise of a drum and 哏兒 imitates the cock's crowing. 草垛 ts'ao³ tuo⁴, a heap of straw, of oats.

TRANSLATION

The drums are striking — (she) is sitting in the chair — and has gone as far the second temple — the east of the temple — and the west of the temple — inside there sits a fat cock — which crows — and flies on a heap of straw.

CVIII

一進門兒黑咕窿咚
先當銅盆後當燈
一進門兒本是一窩耗子精
說一聲不好牆要咕咚

NOTES

The interior of a miserable house is described. 黑咕窿咚 hei¹ ku¹ lung² tung¹ (pronounce with the accent on the last) the first syllabe only gives a clear sense-the other cannot be explained but the general sense is that of complete obscurity, chaos. 耗子精 hao⁴ tzǔ ching¹, transformation of mice: fantastical mouse-like elves. 不好 pu⁴ hao³ here alas!

TRANSLATION

Upon entering all was pitch dark — because first the copper basin had been pawned and then the lamp too — going inside (I perceived) I was in a nest of mouse-like elves — and just when I was saying: alas! here the wall is coming down!

CIX

高高山上一座慺
男人梳着女人頭
狀元及第空歡喜
恩愛夫妻不到頭

NOTES

At first it was very difficult for me to get any sense out of these four verses but at last I got from quite an uncultivated person this explanation which could solve all the difficulties. The words above refer to the theatre and to the actors. In China no female actors are allowed and so the second verse could represent a man who combs the hair as a woman, to act on the stage. It seems furthermore to say in the third verse that although the actors on the stage very often play the part of scholars approved at the examinations yet they have no real reason to be glad there at. The fourth verse then means to say that although loving and affectionates pairs are to be seen on the stage yet that is sham as they are of the same sex. 及第 chi² ti⁴, technical phrase to mean "to be approved at the examinations". 空 k'ung¹, void, vainly. 恩愛 en¹-ai⁴, mutual love derived from gratitude and esteem, as that between husband and wife. 不到頭 pu⁴ tao⁴ t'au², "does not come to a point" that is, has no aim, no regular fruit, as expected after marriage.

TRANSLATION

On a very high mountain there is a high tower (stage) — a man is combing there as a woman — the first candidate approved at the examinations rejoices in vain — and loving husband and wife will never come to a point.

CX

小元兒小元兒
偕們倆人頑兒
踢球打嘎兒
上二閘兒
吃了一個飯兒
喝了一個茶兒
回到家去
偕們倆人頑兒

NOTES

小元兒 hsiao³ yüan²'r, "the small First" surname for a boy. 踢球 t'i¹ ch'iu² to kick balls" sort of game in which the ability consists in pushing with the feet a stone ball and trying to touch the adversary's. 打嘎兒 ta³ ka²'r, another game which consists in throwing very far a wooden ball by mean of a wooden racket called 棒兒 pang¹'r. 二閘兒 eur⁴ cha²'r, the second canal lock near the Tung-pien-men. On the banks there is a very elegant resort for young men. Eating-houses provide meals, female singers, boats and all that is necessary to make a Chinese happy.

TRANSLATION

Small Yüar², small Yüar² — now, let us play — let us kick the balls or play at rackets — and go to the second Canal lock — when we shall have taken a meal — and when we shall have drunk tea — we will go back home — now, let us play!

CXI

裳
衣
洗
白
兒

門兒
娶得
白婦
個媳

花兒
燒一
個大
倒落
有

月亮亮開洗娶不愛愛燒黑倆隔姜也綠
亮堂開得了存喝鬥餅麪大壁三會靴
爺堂堂後白個財酒牌麻火錢兒哥過子

綠 帽 子
綠 袍 子
綠 套 子

NOTES

月亮爺 yüe¹ liang² ye², " the father moon " name given to the moon by children. 亮堂堂 liang¹ t'ang¹ t'ang¹, very bright. Observe here the change of tone in the word 堂 to be read regularly t'ang². 存財 ts'un² ts'ai², to be economical, to put aside money. 麻花兒 ma² hua¹'r, a sort of bun. 一落 i¹ luo⁴, a pile. These words are supposed to be uttered by a wife who in the night, goes out in the court to wash her linen and working, thinks of her sorrows. 姜三哥 Chiang¹ san¹ ko¹, the word Chiang is a family name. San¹ ko¹, means that the man in question is the third in his family. 過 kuo⁴ is here for 過日子 kuo⁴ jih⁴ tzu, to pass one's life, to live and spend one's days peacefully, that is to say economically and frugally. 綠帽子 lü⁴ mao⁴ tzu, " a green hat; the green colour is in China reserved for deceived husbands, and the phrase " to wear a green hat " means to have a partner in the marriage.

TRANSLATION

The father moon — is so bright! — I open the back door to wash my linen — I wash it white and I starch it white — but (my husband) after having married me — is thrifty with his money — he likes to drink wine — he likes to play cards — (and likes too) a great pile of cakes and buns — and brown flower biscuits — which cost two big cash each — but here living by us — there is a neighbour, Chiang the third — who knows how to live well — because he has got green boots — and a green hat — and a green garment — and a green jacket.

CXII

兒活了頭襠脚兒黄穀地
哏賣丫缸褲鍋裏碟面邊穀葉兒裏去
哏垜養個都禿刷洗刷擦洗掃到着上
兒草年八的了他裏他裏他裏他南穀家
哏上一七好剩讓缸讓鍋讓碟讓崩看再

NOTES

From the beginning of the song I could think that the matter is about a cock, but that is only in a jocose way because afterwards it comes to speak of a girl. 裤裆 k'u¹ tang⁴, the bottom of the trowsers. 裹脚 kuo³ chiao³, foot-bands used by women with small feet.

TRANSLATION

The cock crowing — has jumped on the heap of grass — every year he bears seven or eight times — the good ones he has all sold — only a bald-headed (small) girl is left — if he lets her wash the vats — she washes there the bottom of the trowsers — if he lets her wash the ricepot — she washes there her footbands — it he lets her wash the saucers — she washes her face in the saucers — if he lets her sweep the ground — she runs away towards the South to look at the grain fields — when she has seen that the grain is yellow — she comes back home.

CXIII

茉莉花兒丈夫
茉莉花兒的郎
串枝蓮兒的枕頭繡海棠
虞美人兒姑娘走進了房

眼淚汪汪想親娘
臉擦官粉玫瑰露兒香
嘴點梅花胭脂玫瑰瓣兒香
走一步亮堂堂
新買了個小猪兒不吃糠
鼓靠鼓
鑼靠鑼
新娶媳婦兒靠公婆

NOTES

玫瑰露 mei² kuei¹ lu⁴, rose water ; in other cases it means also a sort of white wine. This song seems to be composed of scraps of other songs.

TRANSLATION

The jasmine-husband — the jasmine-bridegroom (is there) — on the wild lotus pillow is embroidered the flower of the *Pyrus spectabilis* — the Rhoeas young-lady enters the room — and weeps bitterly thinking of her own mother — she rubs on her face good cosmetic powder scented with rose water — and she rubs rouge scented like rose petals on her lips — by means of a round cloth shaped like a plum-flower.

CXIV

宮　寺　橋　廟　樓

衣　賣　兒　兒　兒

估　錢　兒　灣　刺　寺　口　糖　房　奶　皮

弓天字塔袍布跳王蘆牌賣兒烟家根國斗街大家袋奶瓜

大朝大白紅馬三帝葫四下多袋毛扎護大新賣蔣烟王西

拉是寫是掛是跳是搖是東衣抽是兒是賣兒安是啃

門就宮就寺就廟就樓就底火就灣就寺就口就房就奶

則去天去塔去布去王去牌牌估火就灣就寺就口就

平過朝過白過馬過帝過四四間個去家去街去家去奶

則去天去塔去布去王去牌牌間個打過毛過護過新過蔣過王

過去就是火藥局
火藥局賣鋼針兒
過去就是老城根兒
老城根兒兩頭兒多
過去就是王八窩
晴天曬蓆子
陰天躓湯鍋

NOTES

This song contains a description of the streets in Peking. 平則門 p'ing² tso² men², the central gate in the west-wall of the Manchu city. 拉大弓 la¹ ta⁴ kung¹, to practice archery using a large bow; lit. to draw the long bow. 朝天宮 chao² t'ien¹ kung¹, name of a temple. 白塔寺 pai² t'a¹ ssu⁴, the temple of the white pagoda. 掛紅袍 kua⁴ hung² p'ao², to put a red coat on the image of Buddha, as people do who have received a favour. 馬市橋 The horse mart bridge. A bridge on the canal. 搖葫蘆 iao² hu² lu², to shake a gourd, as babies are allowed to do, in order to keep them quiet. 四牌樓 ssu⁴ p'ai² lou², a square formed by the junction of four streets at right angles. At each side there is a wooden monumental arch. Two of these squares exist in Peking, one in the east of the Tartar city called 東四牌樓 tung¹ ssu⁴ p'ai² lou² and another in the west of the city called 西四牌樓 hsi¹ ssu⁴ p'ai² lou², which is alluded to here. 估衣 ku⁴ i¹, old clothes, the word ku¹ is here pronounced ku⁴. 打火 ta³ huo³, to strike the fire-stone to get fire. Matches are not yet in general use. 毛家灣 mao² chia² uan¹'r Mao family's corner-name of place. 扎根刺 cha¹ ken¹ tz'u⁴, to be pricked by a thorn, a needle. This phrase is merely introduced for the sake of rhyming with the next verse. 護國寺 hu⁴ kuo² ssu⁴, temple for the protection of the State. 斗 tou³, a willow peck, a chinese measure. 新街口 hsin² chie¹ k'ou³, Mouth of the new street, name of a street. 大糖 ta⁴ t'ang², sticks of sugar sold to children. 蔣家房 chiang³ chia¹ fang², "the house of the Chiang family" name of street. 安烟袋 an¹ yen¹ tai⁴, to fit the mouth piece of pipe. In the afore-said street there is a pipe-shop. 王奶奶 "the old lady Wang" there is a temple dedicated to her. She was a very good and religious woman who lived during the present dynasty and who after her death was thought to have become a saint spirit, so that temples were erected to her. 啃 k'en³, to gnaw; this is naturally purely imaginary as the good lady had lost all her teeth a very long time before. 火藥局 huo³ yao⁴ chü², the powder factory. 兩頭兒多 liang² t'ou²'r tuo, each part has the same lenght. 多 is here for 長 ch'ang². 王八窩 uang² pa¹ uo¹, a nest of turtles; this imaginary lair is thought to give a saucy and witty end to the song. 躥湯鍋 ts'uan¹ t'ang¹ kuo¹, they jump in the broth kettle. These words are purely absurd.

TRANSLATION

Near the Ping-tso-men they draw long-bows — next there is the temple Ch'ao-t'ien-kung — " Ch'ao-t'ien-kung " is written on the temple in big characters — next there is the temple of the white Pagoda. — In the white pagoda people come to give Buddha a red jacket — next there is the Horse mart bridge. — Near the Horse mart bridge, take three jumps — and there is the temple of T'i-wang. — near this temple, shake the gourd — next there are the four archs. — At the east of the four archs — and at the west of the four archs — and under the four archs old clothes are sold — you ask how much for these old clothes ? — you strike a light smoke a pipe — you go on and get to the " Corner of the Mao family ". — Near the corner of the Mao family one is pricked by a thorn — after that comes a " temple for the protection of the State " — near the " temple for the protection of the State " they sell large willow-pecks — after that there comes " the mouth of the new street — near the " mouth of the new street, they sell sugar sticks — after that is " the house of the Chiang family — in " the house of the Chiang family " they fit together smoking pipes — after that there is the temple of old lady Wang. — Old lady Wang gnaws the peel of a melon — next comes the powder factory — near the powder factory they sell steel needles — after that there is the wall — the wall is of the same lenght on both sides — after that comes a nest of turtles — in fine weather they warm that shells in the sunshine — and in bad weather they spring in the hoth-pot.

CXV

紫不紫
大海茄
八月裏　供的是兔兒爺
自來白
自來紅
月光馬兒
供當中
毛豆枝兒　亂烘烘
雞冠子花兒　紅裏個紅
圓月兒的西瓜皮兒青
月亮爺吃的哈哈笑
今夜的光兒分外明

NOTES

The first two verses are the common t'ou²-tzu which has nothing to do with what follows. 海茄 hai³ ch'ie², the egg plant fruit. The Chinese pretend to see in the moon a hare, to which they give offerings on the fifteenth of the 8th moon.

This hare is called 兔兒爺 t'u⁴ r ye². 自來白 tzu¹ lai² pai², " naturally white " a sort of white cake. 自來紅 tzu¹ lai² hung², " naturally red " — a cake with sugar on it. 馬兒 ma³'r, a picture on which is drawn the moon. Inside the moon the hare is sun piling drugs in a mortar. This picture is burned after the offering. 當中 tang¹ chung¹, in the middle. 毛豆枝兒 soy beans are offered to the rabbit, as this animal is very fond of this food. 亂烘烘 luan⁴ hung¹ hung¹, disorderly irregularly, said of the beans on the branches. 鷄冠子 chi¹ kuan¹ tzu, the cocks comb flower. 紅裏個紅 hung² li³ ko⁴ hung², " red in the red " very red. 圓月兒 yüan² yüe⁴'r, like the round moon. The water melon which is called on this occasion 團圓西瓜 t'uan² yüan² hsi¹ kua¹ (the meeting melon) is cut in as many slices as there are persons in the family.

TRANSLATION

Purple or not purple — the big fruit of the egg-plant ? — In the eighth moon Lord Rabbit is worshpped — white cakes — brown cakes — the picture of the moon — is worshipped and placed in the middle — the soy beans are in disorder — the cockscomb flowers are of the deepest-red — the peel of the melon offered to the moon is dark — the Lord moon eats and laughs heartily — to-night the moonlight is brighter than usual.

CXVI

船開就船說
南江下船開了
廟王大個一有南江
尚和個一兒邊一廟王大
杆旗個一兒邊一
戲子對一有年今
山刀上馬跑年過
兒線根有上山刀
藍根兩紅根兩
鐙天朝的搬的男
天朝鐙的搬的女

NOTES

跑馬 or 跑馬獅的 p'ao³ ma³ hsie⁴ ti, circus riders. 上刀山 shang⁴ tao¹ shan¹, lit. " to climb on the sword mountain " is the name for an exercise seen very often in our circuses; that of jumping from one side of a row of standing swords to the other. 朝天鐙 ch'ao² t'ien¹, teng⁴, " the staff looking towards the sky " other feat of desterity which consists in raising one's leg up perpendicularly turning the foot-sole to the sky. 鐙朝天 teng⁴ ch'ao² t'ien¹, the same phrase as before in a different form.

TRANSLATION

We say " set sail " and the ship starts — the

ship is in motion and we go downwards to Kiang-nan — in Kiang-nan there is a big temple to the great king of heaven — at each side of the Tai-wang-miao there is a priest — and at each side a flagstaff — this year there are a couple of theatrical performances — and next year there will be circusriders and " jumping on the swords " — on the row of swords there are four threads — two of them are red and two are blue — the men perform the feat of " the stirrup looking to the sky — and the women perform the feat of the " stirrup which looks to the sky.

CXVII

哥哥哭
三娘也哭
車娘你別哭
車上娘三娘坐齊了哭
的娘稍兒樹
穀兒鐺
拉孩聲
拉女叫等芝掛
　　麻鈴
想我三娘一陣風
想我三娘打門鐘
蒺藜開花蒺藜找
誰想親娘誰知道

NOTES

拉拉穀 la¹ la¹ ku³, sort of a locust. The beginning of the song is hard to translate. In the second verse there begins to be light. 三娘 san¹ niang², perhaps it is meant her uncles wife, the uncle being the third in his family. 坐齊了 tsuo⁴ ch'i² la, to sit together, in full number. 芝麻秸兒樹 chih¹ ma² chie¹'r shu⁴, the sesamus plant. This verse and the following form a sort of 頭子 in the very middle of the song, and it is hard to guess why a bell is spoken of as being attached to that plant. 一陣風 i¹ chen⁴ feng¹, my thought goes as quick as a gust of wind. 打門鐘 ta³ men² chung¹, it seems to me as if I were striking the door-bell. 蒺藜花兒 chi² li² hua¹'r, caltrop flowers.

TRANSLATION

The locust cart and the third brother (?) — when I, the girl sit down in the cart, my mother also weeps — I say once: mother, mother do not weep — wait till the third aunt sits also and then weep — on the sesamum-tree there hangs a bell — thinking of my aunt my thought travels as quick as a guest of wind — thinking of my aunt methinks I am striking the door-bell at home. — where the caltrops open their flowers there you may look for them — only those can understand me who long so for their mother.

CXVIII

三兒
小兒褲子鎖着狗牙兒
小三兒拌的兒
三麼打綢褡兒
小甚洋汗褡兒
青白汗馬穗兒
白騎鍋圈兒
白擰辮穗兒
騎青辮花兒
擰緊邊掖着晚香玉
青左邊掖着蔄康尖兒
緊右白襪子一道臉兒
左魚臉兒鞋一道線兒
右雙
魚
雙

NOTES

The toilet of a young lady is here described. 鎖 suo³, to hem clothes, to work a sort of embroidery at the edges of a dress. 狗牙兒 kou³ ya²'r, pattern of embroidery in form of small triangles resembling dog's teeth. 騎馬穗兒 chi² ma³ suei⁴'r, a row of cut hair left standing just before the plaited hair. 擰鍋圈兒 ning² kuo¹ ch'üan¹'r, small braids plaited on children's heads. 辮穗兒 pien⁴ suei⁴'r, the silk tassel at the end of a pigtail. 辮花兒 pien⁴ hua¹'r, the knots of a braid. 晚香玉 uan³ hsiang¹ yü⁴, the tuberose. 蔄康尖兒 a shoot of *Ocymum basilicum* (sweet basil). 魚白 yü² pai², as white as a fish skin; white with a greenish shade of colour. 一道臉兒 i¹ tao⁴ lien³' r, "with one surface" this means that no seam is to be seen on the socks. 一道線兒 i¹ tao⁴ hsien⁴' r, the two leather strings which come on the shoe are as thin as a thread.

TRANSLATION

Small San'r, small San'r — what dress are you wearing? — I have got dark crape trowsers — and a white shirt — on the white shirt are embroidered " dog's teeth " — on the head I have a row of standing hair — and some small braids — a dark tassel for my pigtail — and the pigtail is plaited very tight — on the left of my hair I have stuck a tuberose — and on the right a head of sweet basil — I have too white socks with no seam — and my shoes have leather strings as thin as a thread.

CXIX

隔着牆兒扔切糕
棗兒豆兒都掉了
隔着牆兒扔磚頭
砸了妞兒的兩把兒頭
隔着牆兒扔票子
怎麽知道姑娘沒落子

NOTES

I do not think that this song can be properly understood by children, but the fact is that numbers of them sing these verses the meaning of which is rather equivocal. It alludes to a man who tries to win a young girl in different comical ways. 切糕 ch'ie¹ kao¹, slices of pudding made with flower, dates and leng beans. 兩把兒頭 liang³ pa¹" r t'ou², " a head with two handles " chinese name for the manchu women's head-gear. This leads one to suppose that this rhyme originated from bannermen. 沒落子 mei² lao⁴ tzu, means literally has not a halting-place, a refuge-and then, to be in a miserable condition, to be poor, not to know where to go.

TRANSLATION

From outside the wall he throws slices of pudding — the dates and the long beans all fell to the ground. — From outside the wall he throws lumps of bricks — and has broken the girl's manchu head-gear — from outside the wall he throws bank-notes — how does he know that the girl has no means?

CXX

廟 裏 的 和 尙 拉 大 鎖
挨 家 兒 搖 鈴 鐺

廟裏的和尚化月米
挨家兒和聲
廟裏的和尚典了道袍　旗杆賣了廟
摩勒的魚兒
廟裏的和尚擱落花生小攤兒
大把的抓着覺
廟裏的和尚睡不大姑娘
想着隔壁兒
廟裏的和尚拿大頂經
跐了脖子怎麼念不打磬
廟裏的和尚燒香打
叮兒噹兒的打茶盅
廟裏的和尚留頭髮
一個字兒的不修行

NOTES

This song is one of the less devotional towards the buddhist priests and is widely sung in Peking by children and grown people. 大鎖 ta⁴ suo³, a large chain which the priests fasten to their neck and drag around when travelling about to collect alms. Sometimes, in order to excite pity and devotion, this chain is made so heavy that the help of a second man is required to drag it along. 挨家兒 ai² chia¹ʳ r, from one house to the other in succession. 化月米 hua⁴ yüe⁴ mi³, to collect the monthly rice. Many families are in the habit of giving every month a quantity of rice to certain temples. The first and fifteenth of the month a priest goes around with a coolie who bears a barril to collect the offerings. 摩勒魚兒 muo² lo¹ yü²' r, a wooden drum in the shape of a fish'head; this instrument is beaten during the ceremonies, and is also taken round by almsbegging priests who carry it on their back tied by a cord. 道袍 tao⁴ p'ao², the priests ceremonial dress. 落花生 luo⁴ hua¹ sheng¹, ground nuts. 拿大頂 na² ta⁴ ting³, to stand on one's head, as jugglers do. 磬 ch'ing⁴, a copper instrument struck during a religious service. — 個字兒 i¹ ko⁴ tzu⁴' r, " in one word " altogether, with no exception. 修行 hsiu¹ hsing², to perfect and reform one's character, as chinese priests are supposed to do in their temples.

TRANSLATION

The priest of the temple drags a heavy chain — and goes from one house to the other ringing a bell — the priest of the temple goes out for the monthly rice — and from house to house he sighs ten times, — the priest in the temple has mortgaged the flag-staffs and has sold the temple — and he does not want either the fish-drum or the ceremonial dress — the priest in the temple has prepared a small fruit stall — (and says) " ground nuts, a big handful of them ! — The priest in the temple cannot sleep — because he is thinking of the neighbour's elder daughter — the priest in the temple stands on his head — but having sprained his neck how could he read the sacred books? — The priest in the temple does not strike the copperdrum — but ding dong! he strikes instead the tea-cup — the priest in the temple lets his hair grow — and does not care a bit about the improvement of his moral conduct.

CXXI

膠 泥 瓣 兒
使 勁 兒 摔
刻 了 爺 爺 兒
刻 奶 奶 兒
爺 爺 兒 戴 着 一 頂 困 秋 帽
奶 奶 兒 戴 着 一 枝 鳳 頭 釵

NOTES

This song is sung by children who play at making mud-pies. 膠泥 chiao¹ ni², the clay mixed up with water becomes sticky like glue. 泥瓣兒 ni² pan⁴' r, a block of clay. 使勁摔 shih³ ching⁴' r shuai¹, cast it with force on the ground. Before the clay is fit to be put into the moulds, it must be rendered softer and that result is obtained by beating the clay repeatedly on the ground. 刻, read here k'o¹ and not k'o⁴, to mould. The moulds sold to the boys in the streets are of different forms and some of them have the form of a man or of a woman. 困秋帽 k'un⁴ c'iu¹ mao⁴, an old round hat. 鳳頭釵 feng¹ t'ou² ch'ai¹, a hair-pin for women; it means literally a phoenix-head pin.

TRANSLATION

The sticky clay blocks — first we throw them on the ground, and then we mould out a gentleman — we mould out a lady — the gentleman wears on old round hat — and the lady a phoenix-head hairpin.

CXXII

祭竈祭竈新年來到
老頭子過來要氈帽
老婆子過來要裹脚
小淘氣兒過來要花炮

NOTES

These words are pronounced while sacrificing to the god of the stoves near the end of the year. 裹脚 kuo³ chiao³, ankle bands for ladies trowsers. At the New-year and the days which precede it, every body tries to dress well and to look his best. 小淘氣兒 hsiao³ t'ao² ch'i⁴'r, general nickname given to children meaning the small impertinent. 花炮 hua¹ p'ao⁴, crackers.

TRANSLATION

Sacrifice to the god of the stoves, Sacrifice to the god of the stoves, the new-year has arrived — the old man comes over and wants a felt-hat — the old lady comes over and wants anklebands — the impertinent youngster comes over and wants crackers.

CXXIII

滴滴滴.
垜草上
養媽他 活獨一個
洗盆金
臥盆銀
聘聘一 到山東克
公個十
婆個十
小個十 叔子管着我
他叫 井台兒去打水
的勒 小手兒怪疼得
上樹 鳥
兒歧 扎的叫
受苦受難誰知道

NOTES

滴滴滴 ti¹ ti¹ ti¹, imitates the noise made by

a chicken. 克 k'o⁴, an unusual pronunciation of the word 去 ch'ü⁴, to go. It is specially used by bannermen and old fashioned people. 小叔子 hsiao³ shu² tzŭ, husband's younger brothers. 井台兒 ching³ t'ai²'r, the well step. 勒手 lei¹ shou³ "to have one's hands strangled" that is to say to hurt one's hands by pulling with a rope. 吱兒扎 chih¹'r cha₁, is supposed to imitate the birds chattering. 難 nan⁴, in the fourth tone, means adversity, trouble.

TRANSLATION

The chicken screaming — flies on the grass-stack. — Her mother had reased only her — she washed in a gold basin — she slept in a silver basin — and then they married her in the Shan-tung — (it looks as if she had) ten fathers-in-law — and ten mothers-in-law — and ten brothers-in-law to watch her — now they let her go to the well to draw water — and her small hands are swollen with the great pain — the birds on the trees — chatter merrily — who knows that I am suffering bitterness and pain?.

CXXIV

月亮爺
亮堂堂
街坊的姑娘要嫁粧

錠兒粉
棒兒香
棉花胭脂二百張

NOTES

錠兒粉 ting⁴'r fen³, an inferior quality of cosmetic powder in square pieces. 棒兒香 pang⁴'r hsiang¹, an incense stick. 棉花胭脂 mien² hua¹ yen¹ chih¹, small cotton strip of cloth imbued with cosmetic rouge, to paint women's lips.

TRANSLATION

The father-moon — is bright and shining — the neighbour's girl wants her bridal presents — squares of cosmetic powder — incense sticks — and two hundred rouge cotton-strips.

CXXV

松樹兒
枝兒掛鈴鐺
親娘賣我在小船兒上
稜子米飯
小魚兒湯
端起飯碗兒想親娘
擱下飯碗兒上後艙
哭了一聲哥哥妹妹誰還想誰

親娘想我一陣風
我想親娘在夢中

NOTES

The first two verses form the common introduction. The word 松枝兒樹 sung¹ chih¹' r shu⁴, means literally a fir-branched tree, that is the same as 松樹 sung¹ shu⁴, a fir-tree. 羧子米 suo¹-tzŭ mi³, a coarse quality of rice; the character is not to be found in any dictionary, but is currently written as above. The words are supposed to be uttered by a small boy who has been sold by his mother to be a small servant on a boat. 一陣風 i¹ chen⁴ feng¹, here, as quick as a gale of wind.

TRANSLATION

On the fir-tree — there is a small bell — my own mother has sold me on board a boat — (I eat here) course rice — and fish broth — taking the rice-bowl to my mouth I think of my mother — when I lay down the rice-bowl then I go to the stern rooms — and I shed some tears saying: brothers, sisters, which of us thinks of each other? — the care of my mother for me has been as fleeting as a squall of wind — but I think of my mother in my dreams.

CXXVI

黃豆粒兒
圓上圓
養活丫頭不值錢
三塊豆腐二兩酒
送在婆婆大門口
婆婆說腳也大臉又醜
公公說留着罷留着罷
燒茶煮飯也用他

NOTES

黃豆 huang² tou⁴, a small sort of yellow haricot (*Phaseolus flavus*). 圓上圓 yüan² shang⁴ yüan², " round on round " that means very much round. The song is taken from the country and that may be observed in some phrases different from the pure Pekinese. For instance the last verse says: 燒茶煮飯 shao¹ ch'a² chu³ fan⁴, instead of 沏茶煮飯 ch'i¹ ch'a² chu³ fan⁴, to prepare tea and food.

TRANSLATION

The yellow haricot — is completely round — bearing a daughter, she is worth no money — just as much as two bits of bean-curd and two ounces of wine. — when we send her to her mother-in-law's house — the mother-in-law says: her feet are large and her face is ugly — the father-in-law says : let her stay, let her stay ! — she can be useful for boiling tea and cooking food.

CXXVII

松栢枝兒
碾子軋
我跟姐姐同出嫁
姐姐嫁在南山裏
妹妹嫁在北漥裏

NOTES

栢樹 pai¹ shu⁴, the cypress. The branches of fir and cypress are burned in some offerings to the spirits, but here the second verse has no rational meaning.

TRANSLATION

The branches of fir and cypress — are crushed by a stone roller (?) — I and my elder sister both marry — my elder sister will marry in the mountains of the South — and I will marry in the Northern bogs.

CXXVIII

一個毬兒

拍兩瓣兒
打花鼓兒
繞花線兒
裏拐外拐
八仙過海
九十九個一百

NOTES

The shuttle-cok is kicked by boys but the girls push the ball with their hands and this is called 拍 p'ai¹. Sometimes while playing they sing some rhymes, one of which I present to the reader. 拍兩瓣兒 p'ai¹ liang³ pan'⁴ r, is struck so hard as to be broken in two pieces. 打花鼓兒 ta³ hua¹ ku³, sort of musical amusement consisting of a song accompanied by drum beating performed generally by girls. This drum beating is accompanied by various evolutions of the arms, non unlike the movement of pushing the shuttle-cok. — 繞花線兒 jao⁴ hua¹ hsien⁴, r, another game. The player places the shuttle-cok on his foot, kicks it in the air, awaits its falling down, and just before it touches the ground, he turnes the foot down round it and kicks it up again. 裏拐外拐 liu³ kai³ uai⁴ kuai³, pushing inside and pushing outside the shuttle-cok.

TRANSLATION

A shuttle-cok — is kicked up and broken in

two pieces — beat the drum — pick up the shuttle-cock. — push inside, push outside — the eight genii cross the sea — ninety nine and a hundred.

CXXIX

梆梆得梆梆
汪汪得汪汪
誰兒一聲
說着毛驢兒
騎着米
扛粗的
要細的
要糠兒的
量淨兒的
簸

NOTES

梆梆 pang¹ pang¹, imitates the knock at the door. 汪汪 uang⁴ uang⁴, the barking of a dog. 毛驢兒 mao² lü²' r, a common name for an ass, instead of the simple 驢兒 lü²' r. A slang word for it is 毛團兒 mao² t'uan²' r; here the rice-seller is supposed to advertise his wares in the last four verses. 量糠兒的 liang² k'ang¹ 'r ti², rice and husks together, rice which has not been winnowed. 簸淨兒的 puo³ ching⁴ 'r ti, clean rice with no husks.

TRANSLATION

People knock at the door — and the dog barks — I ask once, who is there? — (the rice seller) rides an ass — and bears the rice on his back. — (he says) do you want coarse rice? — do you want fine rice? — here is rice and husk, — and here is winnowed rice.

CXXX

小 陶 氣 兒
跳 鑽 鑽 兒
腦 瓜 兒 上 梳 着 個 小 蠟 千 兒
一 人 學 了 八 宗 藝
撞 鐘 踢 球 外 帶 打 嘎

NOTES

跳鑽鑽兒 t'iao⁴ tsuan¹ tsuan¹' r, hopping and jumping. 蠟千兒 la⁴ c'ien¹' r, a chinese candlestick. When boys have not yet hair enough to comb a pigtail, sometimes their hair is bound up in a small plait which stands perpendicularly on the top of the head. 八宗藝 pa¹ tsung² i⁴, eight kinds of abilities. 撞鐘 chuang⁴ chung⁴, lit. "to strike the bell". A game practised by boys who each throw a piece of cash against a wall. The greater or lesser distance to which the cash rebounds from the wall makes one the winner or loser. 外帶 uai⁴ tai⁴, and furthermore.

TRANSLATION

The impertinent youngster — goes hopping and jumping — he has a " candle " toupet on his head — he himself has mastered eight sorts of abilities — he can play at " bell-striking " at football and also at wood ball.

CXXXI

打 羅 兒 篩
曳 羅 兒 篩
該 我 的 麪 錢 不 拿 來
多 會 兒 拿 來
逛 燈 拿 來
甚 麼 燈
小 脚 兒 燈
一 登 登 了 個 大 窟 窿

NOTES

逛 燈 kuang⁴ teng¹, a festival from the 13th to the 17th of the first moon. In the evening lanterns are hung out by shops and private houses. 小脚兒燈 hsiao³ chiao³⁾ r teng¹. A lantern shaped in the form of a chinese small foot. The introduction to this song is identical with another translated before. 登 is pronounced like "lantern" therefore the pun.

TRANSLATION

Strike the sieve and sift — drag the sieve and sift — you owe me money for flour and do not pay me — when will you bring it here? — At the festival of Lanterns I'll bring it — what lantern? — The small foot lantern. — walking on it I made a big hole in it.

CXXXII

姐八的粉搽抹一個兒斜多麼
大十臉兒意脂着角蓮量二寸
小纜滿桃任胭梳鬢金橫
鋸子大疤拉
血絲胡拉
蘇州纂兒
捎一枝花
大八

NOTES

小大姐 hsiao³ ta⁴ chie³, the young lady. The picture is humourous. 鋸子 chü¹ tzu, "a saw" it refers to the fact that after the small pox the skin of the face sometimes is glued together thus forming a scar and a small pimple on it. 桃兒粉 t'ao²'r fen³, red cosmetic powder sold in peach like beads. 血絲胡拉, read almost in one word hsie³ sz-hu-là. I have only adopted these characters in order to write down the sound as spoken; the general meaning is to look as if besmeared with blood — 橫量 heng² liang², measuring the size of the foot. The smallest foot is three inches.

TRANSLATION

The young lady — has just reached her eighteenth year — she has the face full of pimples and scars — with red cosmetic — she rubs all over the face to her heart's desire and then she combs her hair into a Soo-chow chignon — near the temple she sticks a flower in her hair — how big is her foot? — altogether two inches and eight tenths of an inch.

CXXXIII

我的兒
我的姣
三年不見長的這麼高
騎着我的馬
拿着我的刀
扛着我的案板賣切糕

TRANSLATION

My son — my treasure — during the three years that I have not seen you, you have grown so tall — riding my horse — taking my swoard — bearing on your shoulder my kneading-board and selling slices of pudding.

CXXXIV

豆 芽 菜
水 溯 溯
誰 家 的 媳 婦 兒 打 公 公
公 公 拿 着 枴 棍 兒 拐
媳 婦 兒 拿 着 袖 口 兒 甩

NOTES

豆芽菜 tou¹ ya² ts'ai⁴, bean sprouts commonly eaten in China. 水澎澎 shuei³ p'eng¹ p'eng¹, flowing with water; these sprouts are put in water to keep them fresh.

TRANSLATION

The bean sprouts — are dripping with water — who is the wife who dares to beat her father in law? — the father-in-law beats her with his stick — and the woman only lets her sleeve down (with anger).

CXXXV

秦始皇
砌城牆
牆頭兒矮
磴兒窄
擋着達子過不來
後來有個孟姜女
千里來尋夫
對着牆一哭
哭了一聲天兒
哭塌了半邊兒

NOTES

秦始皇 ch'in² shih³ huang², the emperor who built the great wall and who is said to have had buried in it all the men who died during its building. 城墻 ch'eng² ch'iang² " the fortified wall " the full name is 萬里長城 uan³ li³ ch'ang² ch'eng². 磴兒窄 teng⁴'r chai³, the layers of brick are so thin that a man is able to creep on the wall as up stairs. 孟姜女 Meng⁴ chiang³ nü³. A beautiful woman whose husband, although a hsiou⁴ ts'ai², was forced to work at the wall; being in delicate health he died and was buried in the brickwork. When his wife came for him and heard of his end, she knelt by the wall and wept invoking Heaven. She so moved Heaven that the wall crumbled away at the spot and showed her husband's remains: she piously exhumed them, and took them with her. She was afterwards rewarded by the Emperor who granted her a precious belt. But she was so oppressed with grief that at last she ran her head against a wall and died.

TRANSLATION

The Emperor Shih-huang — built the Great Wall — the top of the wall was low — and the steps were short — to prevent the Tartars from crossing — There was Meng chiang nü — who came from a thousand miles away to find her husband — then wept in front of the wall — wept and cried : O Heaven ! — and at her tears the side of the wall fell down.

CXXXVI

蹊蹊蹺 換個牛
換把刀 牛沒甲
刀不快 換匹馬
切青菜 馬沒鞍
葉兒青 上南山
換把弓 南山一窩兔兒
弓沒頭 剝了皮兒穿條褲兒

NOTES

This rhyme has no sense all through. 蹊蹺 hsi¹ ch'iao⁴, extraordinary, uncommon ; at least it is the only meaning and writing which may reasonably agree with the pronunciation hsi¹ ch'iao⁴.

TRANSLATION

Very extraordinary — change a sword — the sword does not cut — hash vegetables — their leaves are green — change a bow — the bow has no head — change an ox — the ox has no scales — change a horse — the horse has no saddle — go to the South hills — in the southern hills there is a nest of hares — from which we take the skin to make a pair of trowsers.

CXXXVII

白 塔 寺
有 白 塔
塔 上 有 磚 沒 有 瓦
塔 臺 兒 上 裂 了 一 道 縫
魯 班 爺 下 來 鋸 上 塔

NOTES

Near the P'ing-tso-men there is a pagoda already spoken of in rhyme Nº114. During this dynasty it threatened to collapse and showed a great crack. The popular tradition says that just at that time somebody dressed like a mason walked round and round the place shouting the words. 鋸 大 傢 伙 兒 chü¹ ta⁴ chia¹ huo³⁾ r " mend the big thing ". A few days after, with great astonishment the candid Pekinese observed that the crack in the pagoda had been repaired and on the fresh work was visible the mark of a mason's trowel. The popular fancy nowhere so wildly developed as in China, directly connected this mysterious piece of masonry with the workman's words and recognized in him **Lu³ pan¹ ye²**, the Genius protector of masons and carpenters. As to the historical truth of the work so well executed, it may be explained in two ways: either the work had been done by government order and at an uncommon time of the day: or more probably that crack had never existed.

TRANSLATION

At the temple of Pai-t'a-ssu, there is a white pagoda — on the pagoda there are bricks but not tiles — on the pagoda's pedestal a gaping crack appeared — and Lu-pan-ye himself came down to repair it.

CXXXVIII

麻 子 鬼
偷 凉 水
搬 倒 了 缸
砸 了 腿
你 賠 我 的 缸
我 賠 你 的 腿

NOTES

痲子鬼 ma² tzu kuei¹, is said jocularly about a child much marked by smallpox.

TRANSLATION

The " small pox devil " — stealing the water — has upset the bucket — and has broken his leg — you repay me for my bucket — and I will repay you for your leg.

CXXXIX

喜 花 搯 來 戴 滿 頭
喜 酒 兒 斟 上 嘔 幾 嘔
喜 鳥 兒 落 在 房 簷 兒 上
哨 的 是 喜 報 三 元 獨 占 鰲 頭

NOTES

The hsi³ or joy here alluded, to is the approval at the examinations. 嘔 ou¹, means to drink, to gulp down. 三元 san¹ yüan²: a candidate who has taken the highest places at the examinations. These words are pronounced by the joy-messengers 報喜的 pao⁴ hsi³ ti, when they reach the door of the successful candidate. 獨占鰲頭 tu² chan⁴ ao¹ t'ou², (the man who has been successful at the last Hanlin examinations is said) to have alone occupied the Ao-fish's head.

TRANSLATION

Here are the flowers of joy, pick them up and cover your head with them — here is the wine of joy, pour it out and drink — the birds of joy come to stop under the eaves of the roof — and the news they bear is : the first successful candidate at the examinations.

CXXXX

錐幫子兒
納底子兒
掙了二升小米子兒
蒸蒸烙烙
吃他娘的一頓犒勞

NOTES

This rhyme speaks jocularly of a little fellow who is supposed to work in order to give himself a treat. 小米 hsiao³ mi³, millet — 蒸 cheng¹, to steam. 烙 lao⁴, to fry in a pan. 犒勞 k'ao⁴ lao², a treat given on some lucky days, to soldiers or workmen.

TRANSLATION

(The boy) bores the heelband of the shoe — and stitches the shoe sole — he has earned two pecks of millet — after a good deal of steaming and frying — he eats a good meal given to him by his mother as a reward.

CXXXXI

月亮爺
明煌煌
騎着大馬去燒香
大馬拴在梧桐樹
小馬拴在廟門兒上

NOTES

明煌煌 ming² huang² huang², extremely bright.
梧桐 u² t'ung², the *Sterculia platanifolia* (Catalpa).

TRANSLATION

The Lord moon — how bright he is — on horse-back I go to burn incense — the big horse is bound to the Catalpa tree — and the small horse to the temple door.

CXXXXII

高高山上一窩猪
兩口子打架孩子哭
孩子孩子你別哭
等着我打那個老丈夫

NOTES

The first verse is a good sample of those extraordinary introductions.

TRANSLATION

On a very high mountain there is a lair of pigs — a husband and a wife quarrel and the child weeps — child, child, do not weep — wait till I thrash this old husband.

CXXXXIII

廟門兒對廟門兒
裏頭住着個小妞人兒
白臉蛋兒
紅嘴唇兒
扭扭揑揑愛死個人兒

NOTES

扭扭揑揑 niu³ niu³ nie⁴ nie⁴, to walk in a sweet and graceful manner.

TRANSLATION

A door of the temple is opposite to a door of the temple — there lives a small girl — with white cheeks — and red lips — she walks so nicely that she makes people die of love.

CXXXXIV

鳥鳥鳥　　要打架
身量兒高　　用手抄
要吃飯　　　要洗臉
先毛腰　　　拿水澆

NOTES

鳥, read here niao¹ and not niao³ — the word has no sense and is purely phonetical. 毛腰 mao² yao¹, the person spoken of being so tall, must stoop down to take his food. 抄 ch'ao¹ (written some times when in this sense with another vulgar character) means here to lift up somebody by catching him under the armpits. 澆 chiao, to water, to poor down water.

TRANSLATION

Hallo! — he is really tall — when he wants to eat — he must stoop down — when he wants to fight — he lifts his adversary under the arms — when he wants to wash his face — he poures water down on it (rather than to stop down to the basin).

CXXXXV

這個人生來性兒急
清晨早起去趕集

錯穿了綠布褲
倒騎着一頭驢

NOTES

綠布褲 lü⁴ pu⁴ k'u⁴, trowsers made of green cloth, trowsers for a woman. The man in his haste had put on his wife's trowsers. 倒騎 tao⁴ ch'i², to ride with the head turned to the animal's tail.

TRANSLATION

This man is very hasty by nature — early in the morning he started for the fair — and he had put on by mistake his wife's trowsers — and was riding with his head towards the donkey's tail.

CXLVI

兒兒
兒肩個太
兒飯了着太窮
兒灣個完抱
榔檳買了吃
兒烟買遶
　　又又

TRANSLATION

The poor woman — folds her arms on her

breast — when she has finished taking her food — she goes out for a strall — and buys betelnuts — and tobacco.

CXLVII

是誰拍我的門兒
小狗兒汪汪叫
親家太太來到了
忙着穿花鞋
褲腿兒又掉了

TRANSLATION

Who knocks at the door ? — the small dog barks — a lady relation has arrived — in a hurry I put on my embroidered shoes — but my anklebands have fallen down.

CXLVIII

大哥哥二哥哥
這個年頭兒怎麼過
棒子麪兒二百多
扁豆開花兒一呀兒唷

NOTES

年頭 nien² t'ou², the crops of the year. 怎麽過 tsen³ mo kuo⁴, how will it be possible to live ? 棒子麪 pang⁴-tzu-mien⁴ flour of Indian corn. 二百多 eur⁴ pai³ tuo¹, more than two pai for a chin₁, a chinese pound. The last verse has no sense and ends the rhyme as the person tries to divert the attention to another subject.

TRANSLATION

First elder brother — second elder brother — with these crops how will it be possible to live ? — Indian corn flour is sold at two cents a pound ! — the bean plant opens its flowers, Hallo !

CXLIX

正月裏正月正
七個老西兒去逛燈
反穿皮襖還嫌冷
河裏的王老八他怎麽過冬

NOTES

反穿皮襖 fan³ ch'uan¹ p'i² ao², wearing the fur coat with the fur outside, to feel warmer. Here the words are said to have a laugh at the Shan-hsi men. 王老八 uang² lao³ pa¹ is instead of 老王八, the old turtle.

TRANSLATION

In the first month, in the first month — seven Shan-hsi people go out in the streets to see the lanterns. — they wear their furs outside and yet they feel cold — but look at the turtles in the river, how do they manage to live through the winter?

CL

小小子兒開鋪兒
開開鋪兒兩扇門兒
小棹子兒
小椅子兒
烏木筷子兒小碟子兒

NOTES

烏木 u¹ mu⁴, ebony wood.

TRANSLATION

The small boy has opened a shop — he has opened a shop with two front doors — with small tables — and small chairs — and chop-sticks of ebony wood.

CLI

小姑娘作一夢
夢見婆婆來下定

眞金條
裹金條
扎花兒裙子綉花兒襖

NOTES

下定 hsia⁴ ting⁴, the future mother-in-law goes to the bride's parents and presents the bridal gifts. After this ceremony the marriage is considered fixed and the girl cannot on any account be betrothed to another man. 金條 chin¹ t'iao², short golden rods sold in the gold-shops called 金店 chin¹ tien⁴. Each rod may weigh generally from one to four chinese ounces (liang). 裹金條 kuo³ chin¹ t'iao², sham gold rods given sometimes as gifts.

TRANSLATION

The small girl — has had a dream — she has dreamt of her mother-in-law coming to give her the bridal gift — real gold rods — and sham gold rods — a gown with stitched flowers — and a cloak with embroidered flowers.

CLII

養活猪吃口肉
養活狗會看家
養活貓會拏耗子
養活你這丫頭作甚麼

NOTES

These words are playfully said by parents to their small daughters. 一口肉 i¹ k'ou³ jou⁴, a mouthful of meat, some meat.

TRANSLATION

If we keep a pig — it is in order to enjoy a good piece of meat — if we keep a dog — it is in order to have him watch the house — if we keep a cat — it is to have him eat the mice — but to keep a maid like you — what is the use of it?

CLIII

喜兒喜兒　　賠了本兒
賣涼粉兒　　娶了個媳婦兒
砸了罐子　　一條腿兒

NOTES

喜兒 hsi³ 'r, may be shortened from 喜雀 hsi³ ch'iao³, a magpie, but here it is used as a common nickname for children, meaning "joy". 涼粉兒 liang² fen³ 'r, fresh powder, is white bean-flour which in summer time is kept by merchants in an ice-box to sell it cool. 罐子 kiuan⁴ tzŭ³, a pot taken around by the bean-flour sellers, in which they keep a sort of sauce to season their ware before selling it to customers.

一條腿兒 i¹ t'iao² t'uei³'r, (with) one leg. It must however be noticed that this phrase also means in Pekinese language " very harmoniously, very peacefully " when speaking of a loving husband and wife: as the two persons were only one, tied one to the other, having one leg in two and therefore with one will and wish.

TRANSLATION

Joy, Joy — sells cool bean-flour — but he has broken the sauce jar — and has forfeited his capital — now he has married a wife — with one leg (or, and he is very happy with her).

CLIV

鼓靠着鼓來
鑼靠鑼
新娶的媳婦兒靠公婆
月亮爺靠着娑羅兒樹
牛郎織女緊靠天河

NOTES

These first verses refer to the ceremonies of a marriage procession, so often mentioned before. — According to chinese folk-lore it is related that in the moon there is a big tree called

娑羅兒樹 suo¹ luo²' r shu⁴ (*Shorea robusta*) on which the father moon leans. The word *solo* is derived from the sanscrit sâla. In the first two verses the word k'ao, to recline, to lean, is used in the sense of to be contiguous, near, in great number. 牛郎 niu² lang² or also 牽牛 ch'ien¹ niu², the constellation of the Herdboy. 織女 chih¹ nü³, the Spinning damsel, another constellation. The former and the latter are placed each at one side of the milky way; the Chinese consider them to be husband and wife and say that once a year they succeed in seeing each other by a curious expedient. The magpies form themselves into a bridge over the milky way (天河 t'ien¹ ho²) and the pair get on the bridge and meet. Many particulars are related about this annual interview; there is also a fantastical play called 渡銀河 tu⁴ yin² ho², the " Crossing of the silver river " in which the adventures and sorrows of this loving pair are exposed to mortal eyes.

TRANSLATION

(In the marriage procession) drums succeed drums — and gongs succeed gongs — a newly married bride relies on her father and mother-in-law — the father moon reclines on the Shorea tree — and the constellations of the Herdboy and the Spinning damsel each lie on one side of the milky way.

CLV

紅得哩	七根鬚兒
指甲草兒	六個瓣兒
藍得哩	晚香玉得哩
翠雀兒	薅康尖兒

NOTES

Pekinese boys sing these words to imitate the street-call of the flower sellers. The two sounds which I have written 得哩 to-li, and occur three times in these verses are altogether phonetic and with no meaning tone or accent; so the first verse is pronounced as if it were written hung toli. 指甲草兒 chih³ chia³ ts'ao³' r (pronounce chih² chia³) lit. finger grass, is the China balsam (*Impatiens balsamina*) with whose red flowers chinese ladies dye their fingers, as the Arab women with the hennè. The flowers of this plant may have different shades of colour from plain white to deep red, and are also called 鳳仙花 feng⁴ hsien¹ hua¹. 翠雀兒 ts'uei¹ ch'iao³' r, the larkspur. 花鬚兒 hua¹ hsü¹' r, stamens and style of flowers. 矮康 ai¹ k'ang¹, an aromatic plant, basilic (*Ocimum basilicum*).

TRANSLATION

Here is the red ! — China balsam — here is the blue ! — the larkspur — with seven stamens — and six petals — the tuberose — and the basilic grass.

CLVI

猜才
奴的
大娘二娘猜奴才
三娘罵我醜奴才
我也不是偷來的
我也不是跑來的
花紅綠轎兒娶來的
瞧瞧奴家的手
金珠瑪瑙一大斗
瞧瞧奴家的牙
從小兒愛喝個菓子茶

NOTES

It happens very often in a family that all the brothers marry and do not live in seperate establishments. All the young wives live together and in order to distinguish them, the elder brother's wife is called ta¹-niang², the second brother's eur¹ niang² and so forth. In this way a system of subordination prevails in the family, and the older wives indulge rather often in teasing the younger ones, The ta¹-niang², this powerful chief of this female clan has a greater authority than all and is consequently allowed to brew the most mischief possible in the family. 猜 ts'ai¹, lit. to guess, to solve riddles, very probably means here to guess, to doubt, to make investigations, suppositions on the woman who is the plaintiff in the song, the youngest wife who complains of having been insulted. 醜奴才 ch'ou³ nu² ts'ai². "ugly slave" a must insulting appellation to a woman who has been legally married, implying that she is not a legal wife but a bought slave. 偷來的 t'ou₁ lai₂ ti, to come stealthily, that is to say come and live with a man without any legal and customary sanction. The same meaning is very curiously expressed in the phrase 手拉手兒來的 shou³ la¹ shou³ lai² ti — lit. "to come taking each other by the hand" that is said of two persons who like each other and without parental permission and the ordinary ceremony take each other by the hand and go and live together. — After that in English would be found "but"; this most interesting particle is wanting here. 花紅轎 hua¹ hung² chiao⁴, "the chair as red as (red) flowers, in which the bride sits, when she is taken from her own paternal house to her husband's. 綠轎 lü⁴ chiao⁴, one or two green chairs in which sit some of the girl's relations to take her to the new home. 奴家 nu² chia¹, a term of modesty used by wives for "I" — 瑪瑙 ma³ nao³, cornelion. 菓子茶 kuo³ tzu ch'a², "tea with sugared fruits, as taken by rich people.

TRANSLATION

The first wife and the second wife play at guissing riddles — the third wife insults me as " an ugly slave " — but I did not come here stealthily — nor did I run away to come here — I was married and taken here in a red chair and was followed by green chairs — look here at my hands ! — I could fill a big peck with the gold pearls and cornelion that I wear — look here at my teeth ! — since I was a child I have been accustomed to take " tea with candied fruits ".

CLVII

小胖小子兒眞有哏兒
你可愛死個人兒
小胖小子兒胖達達
你是誰家的愛娃娃
買美人兒
買美人兒
買到家裏作個看家的人兒
有人兒
沒人兒
不用鎖門兒

NOTES

哏兒 ken⁰' r, no recognized character exists

for this word which means, amusing, pleasant. These words are from a mother to her own boy. — 愛死 ai⁴ ssŭ³, to cause somebody to die of love. 胖達達 p'ang⁴ ta¹ ta¹, very fat and big; observe here ta¹ for ta². 愛娃娃 ai⁴ ua² ua², a beloved child. 美人兒 mei³ jen²' r, a beauty, said particularly of women, but here of the boy.

TRANSLATION

This fat boy of mine really amuses people! — you really make people die of love! — this fat boy of mine how big he is — (now, tell me) whose beloved child are you? — who wants to buy a beauty! who wants to buy a beauty! — when bought and taken home he may be employed in looking after the house — never mind whether there are other people or not — it will be quite useless to shut the door with a key.

CLVIII

高 高 山 上 一 個 牛
四 個 蹄 子 分 八 瓣 兒
尾 巴 長 在 屁 股 後 頭
腦 袋 長 在 脖 子 上 頭

NOTES

瓣 pan⁴, the division of a hoof. The description

of this extraordinary ox will no doubt interest the reader.

TRANSLATION

On a very high mountain there is an ox — which has four hoofs and eight toes — his tail is grown under his rump — and his head is placed on his neck!

CLIX

買 一 包
還 有 你 們 鬧 一 包
大 爺 吃 了 愛 撂 跤
你 們 是 撂 私 跤
你 們 是 撂 官 跤
開 着 的 跛 脚 大 蓆 腰

NOTES

These words are sung by children who want to imitate the itinerant vendors of a drug for professional wrestlers, which is called 壯藥 chuang⁴ yao⁴. Is is made into black pills, called 百補增力丸 puo² pu³ tseng¹ li⁴ uan², "the hundred times fortifying pills. 鬧 nao⁴, is not here in its original meaning but instead of 買 mai³, to buy; the expression is only used in Pekinese slang. 大爺 ta⁴ ye², vulgar appellation for a gentleman whose name and titles are unknown. 撂跤 liao⁴ chiao¹, to wrestle. 私跤 ssu¹ chiao¹, wrestling among friends in a club (廠子 ch'ang³-tzu) where there is daily practice for private entertainment or with the view of entering by means of the examinations the Imperial wrestlers Corps, whose perfect and official wrestling-school is called 官跤 kuan¹ chiao¹. 開着的 k'ai¹ cho¹ ti, all this verse is composed of technical wrestling terms; this one may possibly mean to give, to play a stroke, a move. 跛脚 p'uo¹ chiao³, to kick the adversary on the ankle in order to make him lose his balance and fall. 箍腰 ku¹ yao¹, catching the adversary by the waist to throw him to the ground by sheer superiority of strenght.

CLX

初一初二初三四兒
禿媽養活了一個禿寶貝兒
吃禿咂兒
抱禿八兒
禿了脖梗子
禿腦袋瓜兒

NOTES

These verses are completely devoid of any sense.
八兒 pa'r, name of the child.

TRANSLATION

On the first, on the second, on the third and on the fourth — the hairless mother has given birth to a hairless treasure — who sucks a hairless breast — she embraces the hairless young Pa — who has a hairless neck and a hairless head.

CLXI

你要奢你要奢
你要包金的大耳挖
等着揺銅鼓兒的過來你去拏

NOTES

These words are said by mothers to little girls. The character 奢 is read here sha² which means in country dialect what? and is used instead of the Pekinese 甚麼 shemmo³. The first form is in Peking used only in mockery. 耳挖 eur³ ua², an ear-pick. The women generally wear a silver one stuck in the hair above the left ear. Sometimes like other silver head-gears, it is gilt. 揺銅鼓兒的 iao² t'ung² ku³ 'r ti, a man who goes around in the street shaking a brass drum, and selling hair-pins, generally brass ones.

TRANSLATION

What do you want, what do you want? — you

want a big gilt ear-pick — wait till the man with the brass drum comes over and then go take it.

CLXII

開張把一响爆鞭
排兒邊兩神財福增
坐間中子童財招
增福仙增壽仙劉海兒本是海中仙
一撒金二撒銀
三撒驛馬成了羣
四撒搖錢樹
五撒聚寶盆
五子登科六六順

NOTES

This rhyme is sung by boys who go round on new-year's eve to wish good luck to the families in the neighbourhood and to get the gift of some cash. The style is not altogether su-hua. 鞭炮, pien¹ p'ao⁴ " whip crackers" a sort of fire-crackers which sound like the cracking of a whip. 把張開 pa⁴ chang¹ k'ai¹, " people open their accounts" the shops which have been shut for three, four or more days at the festival of the New-year, choose a lucky day to reopen the shop and recommence business. This ceremony is performed with solemnity and with a number of fire-crackers in proportion to the importance of the shop. 增福財神 tseng¹ fu² ts'ai² shen², "the God of wealth who increases happiness" title of the divinity most respected by shopmen. 招財童子 chao¹ ts'ai² t'ung² tzu³. "the young man who attracts the wealth" another divinity whose image is pasted by shopmen on the shop door. All the following are also names of divinities. 增福仙 tseng¹ fu² hsien¹, the Genius who increases happiness. 增壽仙 tseng¹ shou⁴ hsien¹, the Genius who lengthnes one's age. 劉海兒 liu² hai³'r, name of a Genius supposed to bring wealth to his owner. He is represented wearing a neck lace of gold pieces. 成了羣 ch'eng² la ch'ün², so many as to form a herd of them. 搖錢樹 yao² ch'ien² shu⁴, a fabulous tree whose branches are covered with gold and silver, which falls down when one shakes the tree. 聚寶盆 chü⁴ pao³ p'en², a fabulous basin said to be possessed in former times by a certain 沈 Shen³; this basin had the useful quality of doubling the weight and value of the precious metal laid in it. 登科 teng⁴ k'o¹, to be approved at the official examinations. 六六順 liu⁴ liu⁴ shun⁴, six times six may you have favour (may you find every thing smooth for you).

TRANSLATION

Here is the first discharge of crackers and the shop begins to receive customers — on both sides is exhibited the God of wealth — and in the middle sits " the young man who attracts wealth — there are also the Genius of happiness, the Genius of long life and Lui-hair who is originally a genius from the sea — first let him shower gold — secondly let him shower silver — thirdly let him give you as many horses and mules as would make herds of them — fourthly let him grant you the golden-tree — fifthly let him grant you the Treasure casket — five sons all of whom shall pass the examinations and a sixfold happiness.

CLXIII

天皇皇
地皇皇
我家有個夜哭郎
過往君子念三遍
一家睡到大天光

NOTES

This small rhyme is sung by mothers to get children asleep and to break the evil charm which forces them to be awake. The chinese paste on the walls of the town and even in places of which no mention need be made some words which, read three times, are thought to exert a very favourable influence on the events of the day as regards the reader. These spell sentences are generally called 咒語 chou⁴ yü³ — (the word chou⁴, here is in a good sense, whilst in other phrases it may mean " to read incantations and spells against some body " as in the phrase 咒罵 chou⁴ ma⁴, which means to insult and to wish bad luck to one with ready made words). — One of the most common and powerful spells is contained in the first-two verses of this rhyme, as the words which compose them are considered the most honourable of all the characters. — This spell is jokingly composed as if it were intended to be pasted on walls, and not to be sung beside the cradles of babies. 夜哭郎 ye⁴ k'u¹ lang², in nursery talk means a young gentleman who won't go to sleep.

TRANSLATION

Heaven is imperial! — The Earth is imperial — I have at home a young gentleman who weeps during the night — Let all the gentlemen who go by read these words three times — and all the family will sleep till broad daylight.

CLXIV

竈王爺
本姓張
一碗涼水三炷香
今年小子混的苦
明年再吃關東糖

NOTES

There are two gods of the hearth, the one is Li and is not married, the other has the surname of Chang and is married. These words are supposed to be uttered by a poor man who is performing the annual sacrifice to the God, but has not money enough to buy the sugar required for the occasion, and can only afford to prepare the bowl of water for the god's horse and three incense sticks. 小子 hsiao³ tzu "the young man" here jocularly used for I, the undermentioned. 混的苦 hun⁴ ti k'u³, I am living very wretchedly.

TRANSLATION

O God of the hearth — whose surname is Chang — here is a bowl of water and three incense-sticks — this year I am living very miserably — next year you shall eat the Manchurian sugar.

CLXV

灰斗灰
灰斗灰
就灰
灰斗

頭遍進
還進遍
二遍將
還將遍
三遍進
不進

拿在手
喃在口
看你進斗不進斗

NOTES

This rhyme is sung by boys in the street to insult opium smokers. The ways of poor opium smokers are described. These unhappy people when they have smoked the opium pill take the ashes 灰 huei¹, mix them up with saliva and make a new pill, which they place in the pipe-hole called 斗 tou³. This operation of forming a new ball with the ashes is repeated as often as three times, after which the ash of the opium loses all taste whatever. 頭遍 t'ou² pien⁴, the first time. 將就 chiang¹ chiu⁴, tolerably good, it can be used. 不進斗 pu⁴ chin⁴ tou³, it means " that the ashes are no longer any good, they cannot again be pressed together to form a pill, and therefore they cannot be smoked; so they do not enter the bowl of the pipe. 喃 this character is read an³ and nan³, and means to place something in the palm of the hand and raise it to the mouth; also to stoop down to catch hold of something with the mouth. The opium smokers chew the opium ash when it cannot be smoked any more.

TRANSLATION

The first time the ashes — may enter the bowl

of the pipe the second time — it is not so good — and the third time — they cannot be used — then the man rolls the ashes in his hands — and raises them to his mouth — let us see if this time they can enter this (new) pipe mouth.

CLXVI

三月三誕壽慶娘娘母王年年
有個三月三誕壽慶娘娘母王年年

三月三誕壽慶娘娘有個年年
王母娘娘慶壽誕有個三月三
各洞神仙來上壽
蟠桃美酒會羣仙

NOTES

The third day in the third moon is the birthday of Hsi¹-uang² mu³, the western Royal Mother, worshipped by the Chinese. 洞神 tung⁴ shen², the Spirits are supposed to live in grottoes. 蟠桃 p'an² t'ao² flat peaches. 蟠桃會 p'an² t'ao² huei⁴, is also called the festival in honour of Hsi-uang²-mu³, Every spirit in attendance is supposed to be presented with a peach. See the play called P'an-t'ao-huei. 羣仙 ch'ün² hsien¹, to assemble the spirits.

TRANSLATION

Every year there is the festival of the 3ᵈ day of the third moon — it is the Birthday of the Royal Mother — All the spirits in the grottoes come to assist at the ceremony — the flat peaches and the good wine can make the spirits assemble.

CLXVII

南京大柳樹
北京沈萬三
滄州的獅子景州的塔
深州蜜桃摃口兒甜

NOTES

In this rhyme are collected some of the rarities to be seen in the Empire. 沈萬三 Shen³ uan⁴ san¹, name of the propieter of that famous treasure-basin 聚寶盆 chü⁴ pao³ p'en² which has been spoken of before. 滄州 Ts'ang¹ chow¹, in the Tientsin prefecture. It is stated there is an iron lion, in the interior of which there is room for ten men. 景州塔 ching³ chou¹ t'a³, a high pagoda in Ching-chow, in the Chihli province; it is stated it is very high and may be seen at the distance of fifty *li*. 深州 Shen¹ chow¹, a place renowned for its magnificent peaches. 摃口兒甜 kang⁴ k'ou³ 'r t'ien², so sweet that they fill the mouth; the same idea is also expressed by 殺口兒甜 sha¹ k'ou₃ r' t'ien₂.

TRANSLATION

The willow trees in Nanking — The man Shen-uan-san in Peking — the lion in Ts'ang-chow, and the pagoda in Ching-chow — and the very sweet peaches in Shen-chow.

CLXVIII

轂洞洞
太平車
裏頭坐着個俏哥哥
城外去聽野台兒戲
回頭逛個十里河兒
老爺廟鬧吵吵
人海人山眞熱鬧
村兒裏的姑娘來賣俏
臉搽官粉賽過一個大白瓢

NOTES

轂洞洞 ku¹ tung¹ tung¹, a slang surname for a sort of travelling cart covered with a mat awning- a better name for it is 太平車 t'ai¹ p'ing² ch'o¹. 野台兒戲 ye³ t'ai² 'r hsi⁴, performances on wooden stages in the country, the expense of which is paid for by means of general contributions amongst the peasants. 十里河兒 shih² li³ ho² 'r, "the ten *li* river" a brook outside the Kiang-tso-men in Peking. By its side there is a large temple in which a festival is held on the 24th of the 6th moon: its name is 老爺廟 Lao³ ye² miao⁴. 鬧吵吵 nao⁴ ch'ao¹ ch'ao¹, great noise and hubbub. 人海人山 jen² hai³ jen² shan¹, the men were there as thick as water and as high as hills. 賣俏 mai⁴ cʻiao⁴, " to sell attractions " means " to make a display " to show off. The comparison of the girls head with the white calabash is made in mockery.

TRANSLATION

In the awning-cart — there sits a nice fellow — he is going outside the town to hear the village comedies — and then he will go down to the River of ten *li* — In the Lao-ye temple there is great confusion — the crowd is enormous, and it is very animated — the girls from the villages come here to display their charms — and their faces rubbed with white cosmetics look just like white gourds.

CLXIX

壽星老兒福祿星
增福增壽壽長生
生文生武生貴子
子孝孫賢輩輩兒榮

NOTES

This rhyme is sung by children on birthdays. The three happy stars are the 壽星 shou⁴ hsing¹, the star of longevity, 福星 fu² hsing¹, the star of happiness and 祿星 lu⁴ hsing¹, the star of appointment.

The spirit which presides over longevity is called 壽星老兒 shou¹ hsing¹ lao³ 'r.

TRANSLATION

The spirit of longevity, and the stars of happiness and appointment — may they increase your happiness and your longevity so that you may live a long life — and have sons in the literary career, in the military career and in high positions — may your sons be pious and your grandsons be for ever glorious.

CLXX

小胖哥
玩藝兒多
搬不倒兒
婆婆車
風颭燕兒一大串兒
冰糖葫蘆兒是果餡兒

NOTES

搬不倒兒 pan¹ pu⁴ tao³ 'r, a toy consisting of a round ball of clay on which is stuck a paper man — the plaything is so made that in whatever position one puts it, by the law of gravity it takes again its upright position. 婆婆車 p'uo² p'uo² ch'o¹, ladies carriage, another toy. 風颭燕兒 feng¹ kua¹ yen⁴'r, another plaything in the form of a stick on which a thread is tied, not unlike a fiddestick. On this thread are fixed many paper flowers, which at the least breath of wind begin to revolve causing a peculiar whirring round. 氷糖葫蘆 ping¹ t'ang² hu² lu², some fruits as the hai-t'ang are strung together by a thin stick and covered with sugar; this is called a "sugar-gourd".

TRANSLATION

This fat boy — has many toys — a clay puppet — and a small cart — and a great string of paper flowers — and sugar-gourds stuffed with fruits.

PEKING. — Pe-t'ang Press.

"早期北京话珍本典籍校释与研究"丛书总目录

早期北京话珍稀文献集成

(一) 日本北京话教科书汇编

《燕京妇语》等八种　　　　　　　四声联珠
华语跬步　　　　　　　　　　　　官话指南·改订官话指南
亚细亚言语集　　　　　　　　　　京华事略·北京纪闻
北京风土编·北京事情·北京风俗问答
伊苏普喻言·今古奇观·搜奇新编

(二) 朝鲜日据时期汉语会话书汇编

改正增补汉语独学　　　　　　　　修正独习汉语指南
高等官话华语精选　　　　　　　　官话华语教范
速修汉语自通　　　　　　　　　　无先生速修中国语自通
速修汉语大成　　　　　　　　　　官话标准：短期速修中国语自通
中语大全　　　　　　　　　　　　"内鲜满"最速成中国语自通

(三) 西人北京话教科书汇编

寻津录　　　　　　　　　　　　　北京话语音读本
语言自迩集　　　　　　　　　　　语言自迩集(第二版)
官话类编　　　　　　　　　　　　言语声片
华语入门　　　　　　　　　　　　华英文义津逮
汉英北京官话词汇　　　　　　　　北京官话初阶
汉语口语初级读本·北京儿歌

（四）清代满汉合璧文献萃编

清文启蒙　　　　　　　　清话问答四十条
一百条·清语易言　　　　清文指要
续编兼汉清文指要　　　　庸言知旨
满汉成语对待　　　　　　清文接字·字法举一歌
重刻清文虚字指南编

（五）清代官话正音文献

正音撮要　　　　　　　　正音咀华

（六）十全福

（七）清末民初京味儿小说书系

新鲜滋味　　　　　　　　过新年
小额　　　　　　　　　　北京
春阿氏　　　　　　　　　花鞋成老
评讲聊斋　　　　　　　　讲演聊斋

（八）清末民初京味儿时评书系

益世余谭——民国初年北京生活百态
益世余墨——民国初年北京生活百态

早期北京话研究书系
早期北京话语法演变专题研究
早期北京话语气词研究
晚清民国时期南北官话语法差异研究
基于清后期至民国初期北京话文献语料的个案研究
高本汉《北京话语音读本》整理与研究
北京话语音演变研究
文化语言学视域下的北京地名研究
语言自迩集——19世纪中期的北京话（第二版）
清末民初北京话语词汇释